HOPE
for a
Hurting World

Devotional Readings
on God's Love for the
Poor and Needy

HOPE
for a
Hurting World

EDITED BY
Robert & Pat Gempel
and
Wyndham & Jeanie Shaw

DPI
DISCIPLESHIP
PUBLICATIONS
INTERNATIONAL

1-888-DPI-BOOK
www.dpibooks.com

Hope for a Hurting World

©1997 by Discipleship Publications International
One Merrill Street, Woburn, MA 01801

Printed in the United States of America

Cover design: Chris Costello
Interior design: Laura Root

ISBN: 1-57782-023-1

Dedication

to our Lord who opens doors,
to Kip & Elena McKean for their constant support,
to Douglas & Joyce Arthur for calling us to God's truth,
to the 100,000 volunteers and full-time workers who
bring HOPE to the poor in 106 cities
and 34 countries

Acknowledgments

We want to express our appreciation for the
great contributions of the geographic vice presidents of
HOPE *worldwide* who work alongside us:

Javier & Kelly Amaya
South and Central America

Dr. Moe & Amani Bishara
Middle East

Lawton "Bud" & Kitty Chiles
Africa, Caribbean and Eastern U.S.

Dan & Elexa Liu
China

Mohan & Helen Nanjundan
British Commonwealth

Mark & Patsy Remijan
Pacific Rim

Dr. Doug & Joanne Webber
Los Angeles
National HOPE for Kids

Shawn & Lena Wooten
Commonwealth of Independent States,
Western U.S. and Canada

Contents

A Note from the Series Editors

As the general editors of the Daily Power Series, we are thrilled to add this volume, focusing on God's love for the poor and needy, to this collection. We are grateful for the work done by Bob and Pat Gempel, directors of HOPE *worldwide*, and Wyndham and Jeanie Shaw, vice-presidents for the New England and Continental Europe sector of HOPE *worldwide*, for the work they did in pulling this book together. God is blessing their work with HOPE in remarkable ways. These couples, their co-workers and friends who joined them in writing for this book (and are listed on the contributors page in the back) are modern day heroes worthy of imitation.

Thomas & Sheila Jones

Foreword

Remember the Poor

> A man with leprosy came to him [Jesus] and begged him on his knees, "If you are willing, you can make me clean."
> Filled with compassion, Jesus reached out his hand and touched the man. "I am willing," he said. "Be clean!" Immediately the leprosy left him and he was cured (Mark 1:40-42).

In Boston, on the evening of June 1, 1979, thirty would-be disciples gathered in the living room of Bob and Pat Gempel. Unknown to all but the Holy Spirit, that night had been destined as the beginning of God's modern-day movement. We came together bonded by the common beliefs that the Bible was the inspired, inerrant word of God and that the true believer would wholeheartedly obey every word. Over the ensuing months, the Holy Spirit took away our doctrinal blindness, which had been created by centuries of Catholic and Protestant denominational traditions, and revealed two radical, revolutionary doctrines of the first-century church. First of all, a "true Christian" is a person who makes the decision to become a disciple and then is baptized for the remission of sins. Secondly, the "true church" is composed of only baptized disciples who remain faithful.

God's Dream

Once these doctrines were restored, the Holy Spirit multiplied the disciples in the Boston church. After this outpouring of the grace of God, the Holy Spirit put on our hearts the dream and vision "to make disciples of all nations." Mission teams of disciples were planted in Chicago (June 1982), London (July 1982), New York (June 1983), Toronto (June 1985), Johannesburg (June 1986), Paris and Stockholm (July 1986), Bombay and Kingston (January 1987), Mexico City (June 1987), and Hong Kong (July 1987). God's perpetual charge to evangelize the world was rapidly becoming a reality. Then once more, the Holy Spirit took away our blindness through our exposure and outreach to the third world and the inner cities in the first world. At the 1987 Boston World Missions Seminar, Doug Arthur preached the Word and called all disciples in the movement to repent of our sins of omission and "remember the poor." That fateful evening, a commitment was made to restore "true religion," helping the orphans and widows in their distress (James 1:27).

Initially, two doctors and their families volunteered to lead special projects: Dr. Mark Ottenweller went to Abidjan and Dr. Richard Rheinbolt went to Mexico City. Through the faith and sacrifice of the Atlanta church, an adoption agency was established. In the years since then, Dr. Ottenweller's work in Africa with the AIDS pandemic has been recognized as one of the foremost efforts to help AIDS victims in the entire world. In 1995 he was featured on ABC's World News Tonight as their "Person of the Week."

Early in 1991, inspired by these three projects, the world sector leaders of the International Churches of Christ and I asked Bob and Pat Gempel to officially direct our efforts to provide *hope* to the poor *worldwide*. Their charge was to establish programs and projects that would enable disciples all over the world to focus their volunteer efforts in ways that would truly make a difference. To obey the laws of the land in each nation, a nonprofit organization, separate from the church, called "HOPE *worldwide*" (Helping Other People Everywhere) was established. Today, through the Holy Spirit, the tireless efforts of the Gempels, the HOPE staff and HOPE volunteers from our churches, as well as many more nonchurch volunteers, HOPE *worldwide* has grown to have projects in 106 cities in 34 countries.

True Religion

Jesus said, "The poor you will always have with you" (Mark 14:7). With this sobering truth comes the challenge to determine which of the many needs should be targeted. Usually, the prevailing needs in each nation are obvious. However, HOPE strives to build relationships with the governmental and community leaders to help identify the need on which to focus its energies. In the United States, HOPE's largest effort is known as HOPE for Kids. HOPE strives to educate parents and assist them in immunizing their children by using volunteers who go door-to-door in the inner city. In 1996, HOPE reached more than a million children in 58 of America's inner cities.

In India, HOPE has built 450 brick homes for leprosy patients and their families and has sponsored computer schools for the poor. In Africa, HOPE has built projects to medically assist HIV and AIDS patients. In eastern Europe, Russia and China, HOPE has helped with adoptions and orphanages. In South America, HOPE has sponsored blood drives, and in southeast Asia, HOPE staffs and operates a free hospital and helps rehabilitate former prostitutes through education and job training. God crowned these efforts in late 1996 when HOPE *worldwide* was approved by the United Nations as an NGO with "special consultative status" to the Social and Economic Development Council.

HOPE Unity Award

Two of the most exciting and significant ways the church is helping HOPE meet the needs of the poor is through the HOPE Unity Award and the HOPE Youth Corps. Through these two programs HOPE is reaching out to two very important groups: the most influential leaders in the world and the leaders of the next generation. Two years ago, Steve Johnson, the brother who conceived the HOPE Unity Award, reminded the world sector leaders of one of Aesop's fables. The fable begins with a father who hands his grown sons a bundle of sticks tied with a leather cord. He gave each of them the command, "Break it." Strong as they were, none of them could manage the task, and they handed the bundle back to their father. He then untied it, handing each a single stick, and said again, "Break it." This they easily did. After a long pause while looking each son in the eye, he admonished them, "Unity gives strength."

The HOPE Unity Award is a bronze forearm holding a bundle of sticks tied by a leather cord. Each year HOPE *worldwide* presents the HOPE Unity Award to a world leader who has distinguished himself or herself in forging unity among his or her people to help alter the social, political and/or economic fabric of his or her community in ways that promote harmony and well-being for all its members. Accompanying the award is a full scholarship to one of America's most prestigious business schools, the University of Pennsylvania's Wharton School of Business. A qualified student is selected from the nation of the recipient of the HOPE Unity Award to receive the $50,000 scholarship. After receiving this incredible education, presumably the scholarship honoree will return to his or her home country well prepared to grow into a significant leadership role in helping those in need.

On August 10, 1995, the first annual HOPE Unity Award was presented to Nelson Mandela, president of the Republic of South Africa. Bob Gempel, executive director, Pat Gempel, director of development, and I as chairman of the board, were honored to be able to present the award in person at the home of President Mandela in Pretoria, South Africa. In 1996, Mother Teresa of Calcutta accepted our award for her noble efforts to help orphans and the poor in India and around the world.

HOPE Youth Corps

Through the HOPE Youth Corps, teenagers from all over the world (many of whom are disciples) are provided an opportunity to see and experience life as the overwhelming majority of our world knows it. These life lessons are taught not in a classroom, but by traveling to third-world countries and working daily with orphans, AIDS patients, leprosy patients, homeless families and others whose depth of poverty is incomprehensible for us in the first world.

The HOPE Youth Corps officially began in 1994 in the Philippines. Over fifty teenagers worked and played with the people of Smoky Mountain, the largest slum outside Manila and situated atop a massive garbage dump. In 1995, the HOPE Youth Corps expanded to include two different sites. Eleven teens traveled to Bangalore, India, where they spent every day meeting the needs of the poverty-stricken residents of four different villages. In Soweto, South Africa, a larger group of 130 helped build a medical clinic, comforted AIDS babies and worked with AIDS victims in their vegetable gardens. In 1996, the HOPE Youth Corps brought nearly 200 teens to six different countries (Hong Kong, Ivory Coast, Jamaica, Mexico, Romania and India) to participate in two-week programs with a mission to bring joy and hope to some of the poorest people on earth. These selfless efforts by the teen participants radically deepened their compassion for people and their spiritual convictions. I know this firsthand because my children, Olivia, Sean and Eric, have been fortunate enough to be included in the HOPE Youth Corps for the past three years since my wife, Elena, and I were asked to participate at various sites.

❦

At this hour, God is still calling each true Christian in every true church to practice true religion. This can only be accomplished through our personal sacrifices in time and money and involvement with the poor, the starving and the orphans in our cities. Then, like Jesus, we will touch and let God heal the spiritually poor, the spiritually starving, and the spiritually orphaned around us. Ever striving to have the compassion of Jesus, we will reach out with the true gospel and complete his singular mission—to save a very lost world. I thank God that he is allowing the International Churches of Christ to serve the poor by working through and supporting HOPE *worldwide* as volunteers. My prayer is that the quiet times in this book will not only open your eyes every morning to see spiritually during the day, but it will radically change your life as your heart daily becomes more and more like Jesus.

Kip McKean
January 21, 1997

Kip McKean is the missions evangelist of the International Churches of Christ and serves as the chairman of the board of directors of HOPE worldwide.

Introduction

Why Help Other People Everywhere?

ROBERT & PAT GEMPEL
Philadelphia, U.S.A.

One sunny afternoon in Calcutta, we visited Queen Victoria's palace and monument. The structures stand in stark contrast to the other buildings in this overcrowded, dirty city. The grounds are beautiful, the monument imposing and the palace majestic. Since the palace was not open to the public that day, few people were around. As we walked closer to get a better look, a young girl of perhaps eight or nine appeared, seemingly from nowhere. Her black eyes and hair sparkled in the sunlight as she handed us a card which read in English:

"Please help me. I need money for food and I cannot speak."

As we again looked at her, she opened her mouth and revealed that someone had cut out her tongue. This is a gruesome practice, done so that children can beg more effectively. A nauseous feeling passes through us every time we remember her sweet face. How sad God must be; no wonder he wrote Proverbs 19:17:

> He who is kind to the poor lends to the LORD,
> and he will reward him for what he has done.

Honor God

Jesus' disciples help the poor, just as he did. He and his teachings are powerful enough to help that child forgive the one who maimed her, to help her family learn to make a living and to convict the maimer of sin. Truly, Jesus' disciples are the only ones with answers for the individual as well as for the society that produces the individual. If only Queen Victoria *would* have brought to Calcutta a true, life-changing faith in Jesus rather than

15

the technology to build a palace, perhaps by now the city would be different. Solutions come when individuals change themselves and others to become like Jesus. He never walked by the needy—whether their needs were physical, emotional or spiritual. Solutions come when we wholeheartedly decide to honor God by following Christ's example.

In 1996 there were 5.8 billion people in the world. One half of those people make less than $450 per year. Who will help the needy, feed the hungry, heal the sick, and seek and save the lost? Who will move to Phnom Penh, Cambodia, to take care of the medical, emotional and spiritual needs of these people? Less than a decade ago, two million out of eight million Cambodians were killed by a ruthless dictator. Today only one physician exists for every 9,000 people.

Another proverb is motivating:

> He who oppresses the poor shows contempt
>   for their Maker,
> but whoever is kind to the needy honors God
>   (Proverbs 14:31).

The parable of the Good Samaritan begins with a question: "What must I do to inherit eternal life?" The answer is to give unconditional love to one who cannot return the favor. Proverbs 14:31 tells us that when we are kind to the needy, we honor God. How did you honor God today?

Offer Yourselves (Romans 12:1-16)

Jesus is the perfect example of offering himself as a servant of others. Read through the Gospel of Luke if you are seeking motivation to serve another. Chapters 1-4 tell us of his birth, baptism and genealogy, emphasizing that he is indeed the Son of the living God. Chapter 4 begins with his temptation and his first sermon in Galilee which begins in Isaiah. He reads:

> "The Spirit of the Lord is on me,
>   because he has anointed me
>   to preach good news to the poor.

He has sent me to proclaim freedom for the prisoners
   and recovery of sight for the blind,
to release the oppressed,
   to proclaim the year of the Lord's favor" (Luke 4:18-19).

After declaring his spiritual identity and being chased out of his hometown, he offers *himself* to put these words of Isaiah into practice in his own life. His ministry includes healing, teaching and preaching to the poor, which includes all mankind.

When Jesus healed the poor, he did so unconditionally. When disciples heal or help the poor, they also do this unconditionally and without regard to race, religion or any other of man's dividing prejudices. However, disciples are always willing to share their faith, as Jesus was, with someone eager to learn. Also, we must be willing to offer our bodies to help the poor.

When we were asked to "offer our bodies" to develop programs around the world so that disciples could "volunteer" to help the poor, one of us was willing (Bob) and one was less than enthusiastic (Pat). The answer to this situation: in-depth Bible study followed by walking as Jesus walked—in the garbage with the poor. In Mexico, Cairo and Manila, the garbage pickers will motivate anyone to be grateful and to reach out to help. In China, India, the Ukraine or Cambodia, the pleading eyes of the orphan say, "Why must I be here?" The pain of the leprosy patient and his or her family will change you forever. And then, there are the streets of North Philadelphia, our home city. Perhaps because we live there, the needs seem greatest of all. Where to start—what to do? We must offer our bodies to the Lord and in his service.

- Preach good news to the poor.
- Proclaim freedom for the prisoners and recovery of sight for the blind.
- Release the oppressed.
- Proclaim the year of the Lord's favor.

One of our challenges as disciples is to help the poor. Fortunately, we have projects established in 106 cities worldwide. We can join with those already helping and in an organized way, help the poor. For those not in one of those 106 cities, the challenge is to find a way. Our hearts are softened when we unconditionally give. Perhaps we need to sponsor an orphan or visit the elderly or pray daily to see a way to help. But to be like Jesus, we are compelled to do something.

Promote and Protect the Rights of the Poor

Once we know what God wants and are praying and asking advice about how to proceed, the answers about specific "how to's" come quickly. Beyond doing things ourselves to help, it is important to promote and protect the poor.

> "Speak up for those who cannot speak for themselves,
>   for the rights of all who are destitute.
> Speak up and judge fairly;
>   defend the rights of the poor and needy"
> (Proverbs 31:8-9).

It is easy to walk by the needy. Sometimes when you *try* to help, you are misunderstood. It is even more challenging to defend the cause of the poor. Yet, since Jesus did it all, we are compelled by his love to do the same.

America has essentially hidden her poor in the bowels of her cities. Many suburbanites are afraid to even drive through these sections of the city. Commonly, the "out-of-sight, out-of-mind" phenomenon causes the poor to be forgotten. Many say, "It's your own fault" to the drug addict. The needs of the HIV/AIDS-infected population are also neglected. As disciples, we are challenged by God to "promote and protect" the poor.

Excel in the Grace of Giving

> But just as you excel in everything—in faith, in speech, in knowledge, in complete earnestness and in your love for us—see that you also excel in this grace of giving (2 Corinthians 8:7).

To be able to give is a gift from God. Our faith is developed when we do things God's way and see how he works. Giving is developed by giving more and more.

For the past four Christmases, we have held a party for the needy children in Philadelphia. Each year, we have had more fun because we have learned more effectively "how to give." We also have helped cook and "give" Thanksgiving dinners. As we learn more and more how to give, our own joy, also, grows more and more complete. We are so grateful for the opportunity to give. Our constant prayer is that we all grow in the grace of giving! If we

- **H**onor God by following the example of Jesus,
- **O**ffer ourselves to help,
- **P**romote and protect the rights of the poor, and
- **E**xcel in the grace of giving,

then we *will* Help Other People Everywhere and provide hope to the poor.

Medical Needs

1

Hope for a Hurting World: Jesus the Model

WYNDHAM SHAW
Boston, U.S.A.

I have heard it said that more than 50 percent of all the people who have ever lived are alive on the earth right now. This means that in spite of all the technological and medical advances, more people are suffering and hurting from one malady or another on any one day than ever before. They are suffering from all types of deprivation, diseases, abuses, addictions, emotional scars and personal fears. Some of these are self-inflicted, but many suffer through no fault of their own. They are poor and needy, without hope in a world that passes by, much more concerned for itself than for others. Where can they find hope for relief, for sympathy, for a kind word, a gentle touch, an understanding look? That is the question.

My conviction is that there is only one source of the hope that hurting people long for—Jesus. It has been said that no one cares how much you know until they know how much you care. Jesus changed the world with his message because people wanted to hear from someone who so boldly showed how much he cared.

Two thousand years later the same "Jesus touch" is the hope for our hurting world. Jesus modeled how he wanted his disciples to bring hope to a hurting world. His example can be described in the following ways:

A Dual Ministry

Jesus went through all the towns and villages, teaching in their synagogues, preaching the good news of the kingdom and healing every disease and sickness. When he saw the crowds, he had compassion on them..." (Matthew 9:35-36).

Some fear that emphasis on the poor and needy will hinder our evangelistic growth, and that does happen when churches move to meeting physical and social needs instead of the spiritual needs of people. When this happens, it is contrary to Jesus' example of preaching the good news of the kingdom in the scripture above.

However, it must be recognized that a ministry that does not heal the sick and care for the poor is equidistant from the example set by Jesus. His dual ministry met people's immediate, physical needs by serving the individual and met people's eternal, spiritual needs by saving the individual's soul. Jesus did not do one or the other, nor did he do one for the other, but both with each other. Disciples' efforts on behalf of the poor and needy show a hurting world today how much we care. Then, as they did with Jesus, that hurting world will listen to what we know about God and his kingdom. Workers in the harvest field must imitate the dual ministry of Jesus who met both the immediate, physical needs and the eternal spiritual needs of people.

A 'Get-Involved' Heart

The parable of the good Samaritan in Luke 10:25-37 is not a suggestion from Jesus that we might serve the poor and needy. It is the illustrated answer to the question, "What must I do to inherit eternal life?" (Luke 10:25). In other words, serving the poor and needy is a salvation issue. Those who are going to heaven care for their neighbors day in and day out. We are saved by grace in order to show grace to others. We need to be volunteers for the poor and needy all year.

Not long after accepting my full-time job as vice president of HOPE *worldwide* for New England and Continental Europe, I was driving home from a church meeting on a Wednesday night when I saw a woman walking from her disabled vehicle toward the next exit. I passed her and the exit before realizing the opportunity. Then came the struggle of whether to get involved and be late for my appointment. After asking what Jesus would do, I circled back the three miles it took to see if I could help.

The parable in Luke 10 makes it clear that we can be *religious* like the scribe and Pharisee without being *righteous* like the Samaritan. This righteous man sets an example of a heart that gets involved, and we must follow his example! Notice the practical ways he got involved:

- Emotionally, he took pity on him, which means that he felt something on the inside when he saw this man's needs.
- Physically, he got his hands dirty bandaging and pouring oil and wine on the wounds.
- Financially, he produced money from his own effort to pay for the man's care. (Fund raising has always been a part of serving the poor.)
- Follow-up: He planned to return to see his good deed through to completion.

Do you have a get-involved heart? It's the only kind going to heaven.

The Personal Touch

> A man with leprosy came and knelt before him and said, "Lord, if you are willing, you can make me clean."
> Jesus reached out his hand and touched the man. "I am willing," he said... (Matthew 8:2-3).

I used this passage to preach my first-ever sermon entitled "Jesus the Servant." I was struck by Jesus' willingness not only to heal the man, but to do it with a personal touch that must have thrilled this man's soul. He probably had not been touched by a caring hand in years, but only felt the sting and pain of rocks thrown by those trying to drive him away.

I have found myself afraid to hold my first AIDS baby in Soweto and slow to pull smelly orphan children into my arms in Romania. Hugging a cancer patient eaten up by the disease tested my willingness to offer Jesus' personal touch. In Berlin, Germany, we are starting a project with the elderly, many of whom have Alzheimer's disease and other challenges from aging. They do not receive the personal touch of many who found them more appealing in their prime, but they need it now more than ever.

Little Kelly is eight years old and still wears a diaper and can't walk, talk or care for herself. I have learned to give her even more attention, hugs and kisses than I give to other children. Both she and her parents need to see the personal touch that communicates that I am willing to touch her life—and theirs— as Jesus would. Are you?

Who Needs to Act As Jesus Did?

In Bucharest, Romania, we are working to bring hope to an orphanage. Two of the orphans heard that Jeanie and I would soon be adopting one of their fellow orphans. They came to a church service and found Aileen Hope, the women's ministry leader, to ask this question: "We heard Iacob has found a mommy—what do we need to do to find a mommy?" In our world today there are millions of people who wonder what *they* need to do to get help. For those of us who follow Jesus it is more an issue of what do *we* need to do to get them the help. With the power of God, we can make a major difference in our hurting world. I believe the stories you will read here and the scriptures that will be cited will inspire you to act.

2

Who Will Weep for the Children?

MARK OTTENWELLER
Johannesburg, South Africa

My name is Tholakele (toe-la-kay-lee). *I am five years old.
I like to color pictures. I like to eat chicken and rice. I like to sing
songs. I live with many other children. Theresa and other women
care for us. We play a lot. We get sick a lot, too. I don't know why.
I get "runny tummy." Sometimes it hurts. Many children cough
here, too. Khotso got sick two weeks ago. He went away, and he
never came back. He was my friend. I was sad.*

*Sometimes people visit us. They smile a lot. They stand far
away. They don't touch us. They don't hug us. They don't kiss us.
They don't take us home. I don't know why. It makes me sad. I
want to go with them. Sometimes I cry. Sometimes they bring
candy. That makes me happy. I like candy. Then they leave.
People don't stay here for a long time.*

*I don't think I have a mommy or daddy. I don't know.
Sometimes I see pictures of mommies and daddies. Do I have a
mommy? Where is she? Do I have a daddy? Where is he? I have
Dr. Mark. I call him "Baba," and I run to him. Is he my daddy?
I don't know. I love him. I love Theresa. I love Khotso, but he's
gone.*

*Sometimes I hear people whisper. They say "H-I-V." What
is HIV? Why do people whisper? Why do they call me "HIV"?
My name is Tholakele. I like my name. Tholakele—"found."
Why do I have that name?*

*I feel sick today. I don't want to play. I want to lie in bed; I
am cold, I want someone to hold me. Theresa says I should pray.
I like to pray. I pray to God. Who is God? Where is God? I don't
know. Theresa says he will help me. Theresa says he will send
someone to take me away. No one has come yet. I will pray more.
Maybe I should visit God. I hope I will go see him soon.*

Will You Weep?

"A voice is heard in Ramah,
     mourning and great weeping,
Rachel weeping for her children
     and refusing to be comforted,
     because her children are no more" (Jeremiah 31:15).

There are one million HIV-positive children living in the world today. There are one thousand HIV-positive children born each day. Already nine million children in the world have lost at least one parent to AIDS. By the year 2000 we will have five million children infected by the AIDS virus. The toll on the young children, parents and families is staggering! Rachel (figuratively, the mother of the children of Israel) weeps for her children. Who will weep for the children of Africa? Who will weep for Tholakele?

They Are Chosen by the World

The children of this world have been chosen by the world, by the people, by the sexually active young couples to pay for their sins. So many innocent children are so unwanted, uncared for and unloved. Abortion, sexually transmitted disease, divorce, HIV and its countless orphans all reflect the consequences of sin. The pain, the sorrow and the sadness of all of us descend upon the most innocent ones: the children. Like Jesus, they have suffered the punishment of sin despite their innocence, and we need to accept responsibility for them. Or will we, like Pharaoh and Herod, destroy the children to save ourselves? (See Exodus 1 and Matthew 2.)

We Are Chosen by Them

Disciples provide the most loving and supportive atmosphere in our world. We have the most strength, the least fear, the greatest warmth and the best support network in the world—one that these children so desperately need. That is why Tholakele runs to me. That is why the children run to all the disciples: They have chosen us. Jesus said, "Let the little children come to me" (Luke 18:16). Will you? One million HIV-positive children need you now. Will you let them come?

God Chooses Us

God has prepared us for them. Perhaps that explains the rapid growth of the church in Africa: God has prepared us in advance for the children. He has anointed us to "...bind up the brokenhearted...comfort all who mourn...and provide for those who grieve" (Isaiah 61:1-3); to be filled with compassion and reach out and touch them (Mark 1:41-42); to throw our arms around them, hug them and kiss them (Luke 15:20); and to feed, clothe and care for them (Matthew 25:35-36).

Every one of us can become involved by supporting workers in Africa, by volunteering in Big Brother programs in our communities, by being willing to physically touch those with AIDS, or by adopting an HIV-positive child. Some of the poorest people in the poorest countries of the world are now doing exactly what Jesus commanded. Even with their limited resources, they are reaching out to care for those who have no one to love them or to meet their needs. It is not a question of money but of heart. Are we who we really claim to be? Are you? God has chosen us—you and me—to get involved in the greatest need of our time: the support of those dying of AIDS, especially the children.

The world has chosen them. They have chosen us. Now God chooses you. Tholakele is waiting for you.

3

Kindness Comes to the Killing Fields

MARK & PATSY REMIJAN
Phnom Penh, Cambodia

I (Mark) still remember arriving in Cambodia in early 1992, weeks before much of the U.N.'s 22,000-man peacekeeping force was to arrive. The streets of Phnom Penh struck me as a modern-day ghost town: garbage being blown along the dusty streets, no traffic, and doors gated and locked promptly at sunset. There was little sign of life.

The Dark Ages

Just a few years earlier these same streets were witness to perhaps the worst episode of genocide known to man. Pol Pot and his Khmer Rouge were responsible for the deaths of nearly two million Cambodians. Upon taking control, the Khmer Rouge forcibly evacuated the capital of Phnom Penh with all its inhabitants. Even hospitals were shut down as all were marched at gunpoint into the jungles. In one fell swoop, Pol Pot abolished all social institutions, plunging the nation back into the dark ages.

For three and a half years the terror continued. One of my friends witnessed a family of three tortured to death by two Khmer Rouge soldiers: the father was speared, the baby was thrown into the air and clubbed, and the mother was sexually assaulted with a pole, then mutilated. Another friend, Kim Meng, recounted how he barely survived Pol Pot's slave-labor camps as a boy. Forced to work under the blistering heat of day with only four hours of sleep and a bowl of watered-down rice porridge each day, he nearly died of starvation and exhaustion. He was so emaciated that all his hair fell out. His older brother died, literally worked to death. Mylia, his future wife, lost all of her siblings and her parents.

Grateful to have survived (and finally to have his hair grown back, though a different color), Kim Meng decided to pursue a career as a physician to help rebuild his devastated country. Highly motivated, he graduated at the top of his medical class. Unfortunately, his dreams of healing the wounds of his people came to an end as he realized he could not support his wife and two daughters on the standard twenty-dollars-a-month salary of an uncorrupted physician. In a land where only a handful medical doctors were known to have survived the Pol Pot era, he had to settle for a job as a car salesman.

The Light Age

However, Kim Meng's dreams were recently revived when he was asked to work in a new charity hospital in Phnom Penh called the Sihanouk Hospital center of HOPE. The Sihanouk Hospital, run by HOPE *worldwide,* is a completely free general hospital. Patients from all different backgrounds and locations in Cambodia can receive top quality medical care free of charge. This hospital, which began as a dream of Bernard Krisher and Norodom Sihanouk, the king of Cambodia, has attracted a top international team of medical professionals to train their Cambodian counterparts. This stands to impact all the people of Cambodia, most of whom have no access to quality medical attention. Thus, countless lives will be saved as hundreds of patients are treated daily while raising the standard of medical care for the nation.

As a result of this development, not only is Kim Meng working as a physician again, but he is also the local right-hand of Dr. Graham Ogle, HOPE's hospital administrator. Kim can finally use his training *and* support his family while having an incredible impact in serving his countrymen.

It Takes Many Parts

Just as each of us has one body with many members, and these members do not all have the same function, so in Christ we who are many form one body, and each member belongs to all the others. We have different gifts, according to the grace given us. If a man's gift is prophesying, let him use it in proportion to his faith. If it is serving, let him serve; if it is teaching, let him teach; if it is encouraging, let him encourage; if it is contributing to the needs of others, let him give generously; if it is leadership, let him govern diligently; if it is showing mercy, let him do it cheerfully (Romans 12:4-8).

How did this multimillion-dollar hospital become operational in just four months? Obviously, this monumental task was leagues beyond the efforts and talents of any one individual. Accomplishing this goal required the power of God who used the collective efforts of a team of skilled individuals and medical professionals. Each person played an indispensable part. Heart, sacrifice and faith also played a part. Many responded on a moment's notice, excited to be part of a project to serve the poor. One individual flew all over the United States for months diligently procuring equipment, supplies and medicines. One top surgeon gave up his top American salary to move his family to Cambodia at one-tenth the pay. An internal medicine specialist and his wife gave up their practice, sold their house and moved to Cambodia with their three children in only a few weeks!

What is your gift or talent from God? What can you contribute? Perhaps we are our own worst enemies, thinking: "What do I have to offer?" or "What might I possibly do?" We underestimate the impact we could have. We limit ourselves, and thus God in his ability to use us to be an invaluable part of something much bigger. What can you do? Perhaps you are not a medical professional or a hospital administrator, but you can do something. As one friend put it: "No one can do everything, but everyone can do something." And there is an eternity of difference between something and nothing. Are you doing something, or are you doing nothing? Anyone who does something, no matter how small or how great, can be used by God to help the poor and encourage others to do the same. Talk with other Christians. Ask people close to you what talent or gift they see in you. If there is a great project in gear, get behind it. If not, pray, dream and come up with a plan. You will be amazed by how God blesses any effort. Others will be inspired and catch on. The bottom line is that God expects something from everyone. What will you give to God?

4

Touching Our Modern Lepers

RODOLFO & LYNLEY CEJAS
Philadelphia, U.S.A.

Wilhelm had been a thief and drug addict for most of his adult life. He was the type of person who would come to your home for a visit, and then come back while you were away and steal your belongings. He was a man who had seen it all and done it all. Henry (a.k.a. "the Rev") and Margaret Wells knew Wilhelm perhaps better than anyone.* Henry and Wilhelm used to "shoot" drugs together in the Wells' basement, and Wilhelm would later steal from the Wells home. After the Wells became disciples of Jesus, God challenged their hearts by calling them to reach out to Wilhelm, who was now dying of AIDS. The challenge was much more than simple evangelism. It was to be vulnerable after twenty years of being robbed, to forgive after twenty years of deceit, to love unconditionally without regard to his life-style and to face their own fears of HIV/AIDS.

However, like Jesus with the leper in Mark 1:41, "filled with compassion" they were able to reach out and touch Wilhelm's life. Many dawns found the Wells on their knees as they daily directed Wilhelm in prayers and strengthened him though the Word and their faith. Many evenings were spent at Wilhelm's bedside, in conversations filled with his questions about the miracle of forgiveness and the promise of eternal life through Christ Jesus. For weeks the Wells loved Wilhelm and revealed to him both the beauty and agony of the cross. Throughout his struggle with the disease, Wilhelm always believed that he would be victorious and defeat AIDS. On September 9, 1996, he won his victory. On this warm autumn day, Wilhelm, with help from his friends, walked to the water to be baptized as a disciple of Jesus Christ.

---

* Henry Wells' incredible conversion story and details of the partnership between ODDAT (One Day at a Time) and HOPE is told in Chapter 19 by Walter Evans.

Six weeks later Wilhelm died. Yet his death was a celebration of the victory over HIV/AIDS that can only be proclaimed in Jesus Christ. Despite a life of sin and separation from God, Wilhelm was now able to spend eternity with Jesus. The Wells are a tremendous example of how we must put aside our fears and prejudices and, like Jesus, embrace those cast aside by the world and most religious organizations. Their love, offered to one condemned to death, altered his eternal destiny and gave him the hope of a home with God.

The Hard Facts

It has been labeled the worst plague of the modern era. It is a ruthless disease which attacks every segment of our society. It is an equal-opportunity killer, attacking all kinds of people without respect to race, creed, color, national origin or sexual orientation. Its victims are men, women, children and babies. Although there are many promising treatments, there is still no cure; and the number of people infected and affected continues to grow at an alarming rate. We are in the midst of an HIV/AIDS epidemic.

As of July 1996, nearly 20 million HIV/AIDS cases among adults and children had been reported by the World Health Organization. This represents approximately a 19 percent increase from the year before. It is estimated that by the year 2000, this figure will increase to more than 40 million. Globally, a new person is infected every fifteen seconds. Once thought of as a "homosexual" disease, the overwhelming majority of those infected today are heterosexuals. In fact, the number of cases within the homosexual community has actually began to decrease. In the past year, 90 percent of all new cases have been heterosexual, and heterosexuals account for 70 percent of all cases globally.

In the United States, AIDS is the number one killer of men ages 25 to 44, the number three of women ages 25 to 44, and the sixth leading cause of death in people aged 15 to 24. As startling as these figures are, the numbers are significantly greater among ethnic and racial minorities.

The problems associated with this epidemic are far-reaching and touch many different areas of our society. One of the more significant but less publicized effects of the epidemic is the large and growing number of AIDS orphans in New York City, which has the largest number of HIV/AIDS cases. There are now more than 30,000 orphans. In the next three years, it is estimated that there will be more than 150,000 orphans nationwide.

In addition to the many physical challenges, HIV/AIDS brings many emotional and social challenges to those infected and affected. Many people with HIV/AIDS suffer from the pain of discrimination, isolation, fear, hatred and ignorance. Often, the difficulty posed by HIV/AIDS is not death; rather, the challenges are posed by living with the disease.

The Godly Response

Dear children, let us nor love with words or tongue but with actions and in truth (1 John 3:18).

With our words we can deplore the plight of the AIDS-infected person. From a distance we can express our concern and write a check to further research for a cure. But John tells us we need to love "not with words or tongue but with actions and in truth." In many ways, those infected or affected by HIV/AIDS are our modern-day lepers, and our response to this disease must be the same as Jesus' response to the lepers in the Bible. In Mark 1:41 Jesus, when approached by a leper, was "filled with compassion" and "reached out his hand and touched the man."

Many myths and much fear are associated with AIDS. But you cannot be infected by touching, kissing, sitting next to, playing alongside or drinking after a person who is infected. Their sneezes and tears cannot infect you. Touching doorknobs or toilet seats cannot infect you. As disciples we must be willing to reach beyond our comfort zones and touch the lives of people we may have the least in common with.

What Can You Do?

You can volunteer at a local HIV/AIDS outreach. You can adopt an AIDS orphan. You can reach out to the prostitute, homosexual, transgendered and drug addict. Certainly this kind of effort needs to be made with help and direction. Pray about where to start. Get advice from the best people you know. You can love the sinner and hate the sin. You can overcome your own fears of this disease and get tested to see if you have the HIV virus. You can offer to have a Bible study at one of the local hospices. You can hug someone; you can care; you can heal; you can invite someone to church; you can study the Bible; you can baptize; you can change the destiny of someone's life; you can arrange for someone to meet Wilhelm in heaven. Most of all, you can "love with actions and in truth."

5

Third-World Needs—
First-Rate Compassion

DAVID & KIMI TRAVER
Phnom Penh, Cambodia

She was born into a world where the arms of her loving mother eagerly waited to embrace her. Like many newborn babies, she was one for whom her family carried hopes for a bright future. But Juliette's world was harsh and one which was not ready to accept a new life. Every day, as part of their routine, Juliette's parents scrounged the heaps of garbage surrounding their cardboard shack in search of any material of value which they could retrieve. These scavenged materials were then sold to a recycler for a paltry sum of money. It barely earned their family's food, but it was all they knew. Juliette's birth provided new hope and joy, and for a while her family was lifted above their daily despair.

However, on the baby's second day of life, Juliette's mother noticed her fever. It soon worsened and Juliette turned a frightening red color. Within twenty-four hours, Juliette's body was tense, and she was struggling to breathe. Within a day, she would be dead. Her family would never realize that it was the rusty razor blade they used to cut her umbilical cord which stole her life and her family's joy.

Juliette is but one of thousands of reasons why Manila, Philippines, needs people who bring hope.

Compassion on the Crowds

When Jesus landed and saw a large crowd, he had compassion on them and healed their sick.

As evening approached, the disciples came to him and said, "This is a remote place, and it's already getting late. Send the crowds away, so they can go to the villages and buy themselves some food."

Jesus replied, "They do not need to go away. You give them something to eat."

"We have here only five loaves of bread and two fish," they answered.

"Bring them here to me," he said. And he directed the people to sit down on the grass. Taking the five loaves and the two fish and looking up to heaven, he gave thanks and broke the loaves. Then he gave them to the disciples, and the disciples gave them to the people. They all ate and were satisfied, and the disciples picked up twelve basketfuls of broken pieces that were left over. The number of those who ate was about five thousand men, besides women and children (Matthew 14:14-21).

When Jesus saw the needs of the crowd, his heart went out to them. When the disciples saw the needs, they dismissed the crowd to take care of themselves. Jesus, in compassion, redirected the disciples' thoughts: "They do not need to go away. You give them something to eat." He told *them* to take responsibility, to search for a way to give to those who were hurting. He got in touch with needs, and used his power to meet those needs.

In the spirit of Jesus, four years ago HOPE *worldwide* arrived to meet needs in Manila in the form of medical relief. Although certain sections of Manila, the Philippines' capital city, have first-world standards, the vast majority of the nation's people live well below the poverty line. first- and third-world families are often neighbors, living only a street's breadth apart. While many of us in the Western world would consider it an outrage to be denied access to medical care in a life-threatening emergency, such is not the case in most of the developing world. Millions of families in the Philippines live with the sober knowledge that should a medical emergency arise, they are at the mercy of the disease's course, which, in many instances, leads to death. They simply cannot afford medical help.

HOPE was ushered into the Philippines in 1992 by the now infamous Ormoc landslide on the island of Leyte and the eruption of the Mt. Pinatubo volcano. As a result of these natural disasters, thousands lost their lives. The many victims of not-so-infrequent natural disasters, however, represent only a fragment of the needy in the Philippines.

Due to the extensive garbage dumps dotting the capital city, HOPE's first project was to set up mobile medical clinics in eight of the most "depressed areas" in Manila. Each of these represented the work of one of the original eight sectors of the Manila church. These mobile clinics served perhaps a million individuals who lived among the mountains of garbage, and who made their living by sorting through the piles to find recyclable materials to sell.

From these beginnings have sprung the ongoing and expanding medical clinics of HOPE for Manila, as well as an extensive social assistance arm of HOPE. This arm includes a home for street children, several training programs and even an educational aspect—a new school and associated tutorials to give the children an opportunity to receive an education.

God has worked through an intensely dedicated team of workers to enable Manila to become one of HOPE's landmark works for the developing world. The native volunteers have poured out their hearts and lives to ensure the success of the HOPE work. Although most grew up side by side with poor people, they have not allowed a callous disregard to stop them from helping those in need. The challenge for us is the same. Let us never allow ourselves to "get used to" the poor, but may we always extend our hearts and hands to the needy.

Jesus looked at the crowd through the eyes of the God who made each of them as an individual. He was eager to meet their physical needs and their spiritual needs. Can his followers do any less?

6

Receiving So Much More Than We Give

GRAHAM & HELEN OGLE
Phnom Penh, Cambodia

We first met Samson in Port Moresby when he was about sixteen years old. Birth records have only recently been kept in the remote highlands of Papua New Guinea, where he was born. He is the oldest child in his family, and the only one to attend school (four years of primary school before poverty forced him to quit). His father was uncommunicative and distant, and his mother was downtrodden and desperately poor, with one ragged dress to her name. His future was bleak in this city characterized by 50 percent unemployment, gangs and violence.

A New Man: The Fruit of Love

However, Samson became a Christian, and his life was transformed. Soon he was coming to our busy medical clinic every day to help out, doing whatever needed to be done. His joyful and willing spirit was so outstanding that when we opened our first preschool, we offered him a paid position as an assistant teacher. He and his family were astonished that we would even consider him. He immediately began to assist his family financially. A few weeks into his job he came to us asking for a $420 advance (two months pay) to buy a house for his family of seven. I (Graham) was taken aback, but went with him to see the house. They were currently living in a wooden shack about the size of a typical American bathroom. The house next door, three times as big, was for sale. I was deeply moved by Samson's love for his family. We advanced him the money, he bought the house, and has since paid back the loan. He has thrived in his job at the preschool and is now training to be a teacher.

Soon after moving to their new house, his mother became a Christian, blossoming like a flower. Then his uncle and his father also became Christians. Samson saw the needs of the poor in his city and his own family, and he did something about it. He acted to meet their needs out of love, spending himself and all he had, and God blessed him.

"If you do away with the yoke of oppression,
    with the pointing finger and malicious talk,
and if you spend yourselves in behalf of the hungry
    and satisfy the needs of the oppressed,
then your light will rise in the darkness,
    and your night will become like the noonday.
The LORD will guide you always;
    he will satisfy your needs in a sun-scorched land
    and will strengthen your frame.
You will be like a well-watered garden,
    like a spring whose waters never fail" (Isaiah 58:9b-11).

Spending Ourselves

God cares for the oppressed. God cares for the poor, and he asks us to do the same. In third-world countries the poor and oppressed are clearly visible. But do not be deceived; they are just as common in wealthy countries: impoverished families struggling in the inner city, single mothers burdened to their limits, adolescents without role models, lonely young men and women, neglected elderly, those with psychiatric or social problems or those in jail.

Spending ourselves means giving our all to meet the needs of others. We can only do this by staying close to God. What does close to God mean? It means a daily decision to keep a willing heart, to do whatever it may take and to die to self. It takes struggling daily against our own sinful, selfish, comfort-loving nature. It takes giving and then giving again. It takes true love for people—looking for the deeper, less obvious needs, avoiding apathy or complacency, persevering in communication until we hit the right wavelength. And it takes loving all the more when behavior or attitudes make people difficult to love. It takes gratefulness for all the blessings that God has given us and continues to give us. Finally, it takes trusting God that he has put us and our families in exactly the right place at exactly the right time (Acts 17:26-27) and that he does this to fulfill his purpose (for which he provides the capability).

When we moved to Port Moresby in 1993, we went with some regrets and some trepidation. In Sydney, Australia, we had everything: interesting and lucrative medical careers, long-standing and deep relationships in the church, proximity to our families, a comfortable and safe Western life-style. In Port Moresby, though, we and one sister from Papua New Guinea, named Ursula Kolkolo were the church. Our firstborn, only nine-months-old, now lived in an environment rife with malaria and typhoid. The city was infamous for violent crime. The public transport stopped at 6:00 P.M., and no street was safe to walk at night.

But the Lord blessed our every step. He provided positions at the hospital and the university, so that we could contribute, and also develop both contacts and later HOPE medical programs in the settlements. If doors needed opening, God didn't just open them a crack—he threw them wide open. Arduous things—government cooperation, private sector assistance and community relationships—all came our way with amazing ease. The church grew and grew.

We spent ourselves on behalf of the poor, hungry and oppressed. There were times of danger, of homesickness and of concern. Times when our children were sick. Times of disappointments and frustrations. We experienced relatives questioning our sanity and late nights spent with seemingly endless budgeting, accounting and reporting. There were challenges to our selfish natures: learning another foreign language, welcoming poor and filthy people into our home with open arms, parting with possessions and struggling to find common ground on which to build friendships.

But, oh, the blessings and times of joy. God always did guide us. He did satisfy our every need. He did strengthen our frames. Our family was like a well-watered garden. He also blessed us with a beautiful girl and another baby on the way. We developed extraordinary relationships with Papua New Guineans, some of which will last for eternity.

Now, we have just moved to Phnom Penh, Cambodia, to establish the Sihanouk Hospital center of HOPE. There are new challenges here, but we know the Lord. He is protecting, supporting and blessing the staff and the project. We are frequently embarrassed when others praise us, because the truth is we have received and enjoyed so much more than we have ever sacrificed (Mark 10:29-31).

Have the heart of God. Imitate Christ. Spend yourselves on behalf of others; don't just put in a check. Don't just give your money; give your time. Satisfy their physical, emotional and spiritual needs. We cannot imagine how far-reaching the consequences of our small sacrifice will be, but to God will be the glory!

Poverty, Hunger
and Abuse

7

I Was Hungry!

DOUGLAS JACOBY
Washington D.C., U.S.A.

The plight of the poor and needy is a frightening one, and often followers of Jesus Christ do not know how to react. For the first ten years of my Christian life, my attitude was "spiritual needs are more important than physical needs." Although in one sense this is true, it also played into my own convenience. I can remember arguing in seminary with a man who reminded me that the Bible commands us to fight for the rights of the poor. "That's Old Testament," I adamantly proclaimed. "Under the New Testament we have *permission* to help the poor, but no *commission.*" Needless to say, that man was not greatly impressed with my spirituality. Before studying what the Scriptures teach about poverty and how I should respond, I blocked the horrors of the needy out of my mind, focused on the "spiritual," refused to give to beggars, and hermetically sealed my heart off from the reality of a world in need.

Everything changed once I went to Calcutta, a city of 12 million, built to accommodate one million. The excess population literally overflows into the streets, which are home to numberless men, women and children. I spent that first night awake, sitting on the floor, stunned. The shock of my first real exposure to staggering poverty jolted loose the barricade I had put in front of my heart. At last I was free to read the Bible without the presupposition that I had the correct interpretation of the Christian response to poverty. I want to share with you what I learned.

Gospel Truth

I discovered that everywhere—in both the Old and New Testaments—we are encouraged time and time again to remember the needy. Of the scores of passages dealing with the subject,

I was deeply convicted by such verses as Deuteronomy 15:4-5, 11; Isaiah 58:6-10; Amos 6:1a, 4-7 and Ezekiel 16:49. My heart was bombarded over and over by the clear teaching of Proverbs 3:27-28, 14:31, 19:17, 21:13, 28:27, 30:7-9, 31:8-9. But this wasn't only an Old Testament teaching! Of the gospels, Luke has the greatest emphasis on poverty and wealth: (3:10-11, 6:20b, 6:24-25a, 6:30-31, 35, 10:25-37, 12:33-34, 16:19-24). Acts follows suit: (2:44-45, 4:32-35, 6:1-7, 9:36, 11:27-30, 10:1-2, 4b…), and then there were all those passages in the letters, like James 2:14-26 and Galatians 2:10. One passage that speaks with perfect clarity is Luke 10:25-37, otherwise known as the Parable of the Good Samaritan.

The 'Good' Samaritan

Jesus never actually calls this man "good." That's *our* adjective. Is it because by contrast we are *not* so good that we elect to call the hero of the story "good"? Please read Luke 10:25-37 and let its words penetrate your heart.

After the priest and Levite passed by the wounded man, the Samaritan "took pity on him":

> "He went to him and bandaged his wounds, pouring on oil and wine. Then he put the man on his own donkey, took him to an inn and took care of him. The next day he took out two silver coins and gave them to the innkeeper. 'Look after him,' he said, 'and when I return, I will reimburse you for any extra expense you may have.'
>
> "Which of these three do you think was a neighbor to the man who fell into the hands of robbers?" The expert in the law replied, "The one who had mercy on him." Jesus told him, "Go and do likewise" (Luke 10:34-37).

This parable contains a plethora of principles on meeting the needs of the poor. Let's look at the situation:

1. *The Samaritan was aware of a need.* The victim had a raw deal. So do those in the world today born into limited opportunity, poverty, decadence. Through the mass media most of us, too, are aware of their needs; we cannot plead ignorance. Neither could the priest and the Levite.

2. *The race of the victim was irrelevant to the Samaritan.*
Even though the victim was a Jew, the Samaritan hero did not let
that prejudice his love for his neighbor. How many of us would
react differently if the disadvantaged of the world belonged to
our own comfortable social and racial set? Do we allow differences of skin color and other outward features to distance us
from the world of human suffering?

3. *Others were not meeting his needs.* The ones who had the
least excuse, here representing respectable religion, actively went
out of their way to avoid the pangs of conscience that might have
led them to imitate the merciful God they claimed to know.

4. *The victim could not help himself.* He was in no position
to help himself. There are countless millions—hundreds of
millions!—who are in legitimate need. Unless we help them, it
is unlikely anyone will. The various relief organizations barely
begin to meet their needs. We cannot excuse our inactivity with
the rationalization that others are getting the job done.

This, then, is the situation. What does the Samaritan do?

- He sees the need.
- He takes pity on his neighbor, his fellow human being.
- He provides medical care and meets physical needs.
- He gives money to a responsible agency (the inn-
  keeper).
- He does not limit his liability, but is willing to "go the
  extra mile."

When it comes to meeting the needs of the world's poor, Jesus
bids us "Go and do likewise."

Where Do I Start?

Where do we go from here? Here are some suggestions:

1. Study out all the verses you can find on money and
   wealth.
2. Sell some of your possessions, as Jesus taught in Luke
   12:33.
3. Scrutinize your expenses. When tempted to make a
   purchase, ask yourself these four questions:

- Do I really need it?
- Would I buy it one month from now?
- Can I buy it somewhere else for less?
- Does it appeal to my status-seeking ego?

4. Make a budget, and stick to it! Decide how much you need to live on, balance your checkbook, and determine to become disciplined with your personal finances.

5. Fast regularly to maintain awareness of the dire straits of the poor. It will add concentration and pungency to your prayers.

6. Consider adopting a child, as we were privileged to do.

7. Pray: right now! Tell God how you feel about these things and what you plan to do about it. Keep your resolve fresh. Ask God to make it clear if he wants you to dedicate your life to a career of helping the poor and needy.

Our Lord said in Matthew 25:35, in the familiar parable of the sheep and goats, "I was hungry." As we reach out and meet the needs of others, we feed Jesus himself. The question is, "Are we?"

8
Comfort My People

JAVIER & KELLY AMAYA
Mexico City, Mexico

Imagine climbing up the Andes in Argentina and watching the sun go down behind the mountains, or scuba diving off the shore of Mexico, the clear waters full of colorful sea life. What about horseback riding on the beach of Costa Rica alongside the great Pacific Ocean or simply relaxing under a palm tree in Brazil. This is Latin America.

Sad Sites

Now take off the sunglasses and see the shocking reality of another Latin America. Have a look at life through the eyes of Lupita, a Mexican woman with a tragic story to tell.

As far back as I can remember, since we were kids, my mother would swear, scream and slap us. Many times she would not give us anything to eat. She would say it was my brother's and my fault that our father didn't love her! I used to think that maybe by obeying her I could get my mom to love me, but often in anger and desperation she would say, "I can't stand you nor will I ever, no matter what you do."

Born in Veracruz, a small city on the Mexican coast, Lupita was six years old when she came to Mexico City with her mom and younger brother in search of their father. They found him married and completely indifferent to them. Two years later her mother got married and left Lupita at her father's house to get rid of her. Since she was unwanted there, Lupita was forced to live on the streets. Lupita recalls her youth when for years all she desired was a safe place to stay.

Her nomadic street life eventually led Lupita to seek the comfort and protection of men. She had multiple relationships and was sexually abused often by one man for two years. Finally,

Lupita met a store manager who began courting her, and she believed that with him it would be different. However, when she moved in with him, she became a victim of his private beatings and public humiliations (he once dragged her through the street by her hair). By the time they had had two children together, she felt trapped in the relationship. He would use the children to threaten and manipulate her saying that if she left him, he would keep the children. He even made good on his threat and took the kids from her, but Lupita fought back and finally took the children and left him for good.

Desperation, hunger and fear were her companions. Twice she was threatened with death during rape attempts, but both times she escaped. She worked short-lived jobs with circuses, markets, street vendors; and she even worked as a garbage collector. However, she became more desperate when she found herself and her children without hopes of a job, food or shelter. "It was at this time," Lupita says sadly, "that I had to resort to prostitution."

Thinking things could not get any worse, Lupita got involved with another man. Again she found herself in a long-term abusive relationship. She had two more children who themselves years later would beg her to leave. "Mom, we're scared for your life. Why can't we leave before he kills you?" This man would threaten her and force her to buy and sell drugs for him, even forcing her to sell them at a prison, risking both her life and freedom. Things got so bad that she ended up in a hospital when he broke a bottle over her head. Finally, his behavior forced her to take the children and flee for help.

> Many times I sought help from those around me, but every time I would end up worse off. After the two years of abuse, I told my aunt and mother about it and was cussed and slapped and told I was a liar. However, deep within me I constantly would pray to God, seeking his help even though I felt so guilty about my life.

Years went by, and she and a new man, Francisco, started living together. During this time Lupita found work in a neighborhood market. It was there that God's hand would begin to turn her life around. She met disciples from the Church of Christ who cared for both her physical and spiritual needs. "They not only gave me a job but they began to teach me about God and a brand new way of living. I learned there was real hope in the world." Francisco and she were married, became disciples of Jesus and are now learning to live a new Christian life together. They are even teaching others how to rebuild a life with a bright future— no matter how dark the past!

Today, we find Lupita at the age of 35, carrying her grandson out of the hospital. Even though he is only one month old and just had surgery to connect his throat to the rest of his digestive system, his parents have abandoned him. However, this little infant has the hope of a lifetime because his grandparents, Francisco and Lupita, want to provide him with a different world than the one they knew. They believe that with them the chain of indifference, abuse and neglect can end. They are grateful to God because, as Lupita says, "My life has been hard, but God has protected me throughout." Thanks to the hope that the disciples have provided, Lupita and her husband can now forge a chain of love instead of hatred, of light instead of darkness, of hope instead of despair.

Looking to Comfort

This is but one glimmer of light.

> Comfort, comfort my people, says your God.
> He gives strength to the weary
> and increases the power of the weak.
> Even youths grow tired and weary,
> and young men stumble and fall;
> but those who hope in the LORD
> will renew their strength.
> They will soar on wings like eagles;
> they will run and not grow weary,
> they will walk and not be faint (Isaiah 40:1, 29-31).

There are many "Lupitas" in our lives. If we are willing to walk around our neighborhoods, schools, and workplaces, taking off our blinders of selfishness, indifference and self-pity, we will see a striking reality around us. If we care to be involved and consumed with the lives of others, we will be able to bring bright light to a very dark place.

God cries out for someone to comfort his people. He has not called you to be comforted but to comfort. He has called you to be his ears and hear those who are crying out. There are those around you that are so tired and so weary of life. Life has pounded them down to the point of hopelessness. It is up to us to be God's hands strengthening them and believing that they can not only get up and walk again, but even soar on the victorious wings of God. Let us have eyes that see, hearts that feel and hands that respond to the "Lupitas" in our hurting world.

9

Through Third-World Eyes

GUILLERMO ADAME
San Diego, U.S.A.

Ashamed and embarrassed was all I could feel as I arrived home with seven visiting disciples from India. We had all just attended a world missions seminar in Los Angeles. As I showed them around, I found myself making excuses for the house that Terry, my three children and I had moved into a few months earlier.

I thought to myself how comfortable I had become living in the Western world. As I began to show them my "average four-bedroom house" they began to make innocent comments that ripped through my heart like flaming arrows. "Your garage is nicer than most homes Indians live in, and it's only for the car." "You have carpeting on your floors—only the nicest hotels in India have carpeting." "I can't believe you have machines for both washing and drying the clothes." "Your television is so big!" "Your house is like a palace!" Then there was the micro-wave, dishwasher, cordless telephone, electric stove, CD player, computer, fax machine and the list goes on. All of these items are virtually unheard of by the majority of Indians. They were amazed that the electricity stayed on all of the time and that there was a never-ending supply of hot and cold water. (Blackouts and water shortages are common daily occurrences in India.)

The item that amazed them the most, however, is something that I don't think much about: the garbage disposal. They had never seen this appliance or even knew such a thing existed. "It's a machine that grinds all of your food scraps so that they will go down the drain," I said to explain its importance. "In India they told me, "many thousands survive only by sifting through all of the filthy rubbish that others throw away." I had a pit in my stomach! I was disgusted with myself! Why?

A Poor Response

What good is it, my brothers, if a man claims to have faith but has no deeds? Can such faith save him? Suppose a brother or sister is without clothes and daily food. If one of you says to him, "Go, I wish you well; keep warm and well fed," but does nothing about his physical needs, what good is it? In the same way, faith by itself, if it is not accompanied by action, is dead (James 2:14-17).

My heart for the poor had become so hard. I hadn't done anything to help the poor in months. I once had a heart for the poor. I wanted it back. James tells us that if we don't put our faith into action then our faith is dead!

I had hurt God by my hardness. I was convicted by the book of Proverbs: "If a man shuts his ears to the cry of the poor, he too will cry out and not be answered" (Proverbs 21:3). I needed back the heart I had when I had been on the mission team in Bombay, India.

We had taken up the "one suitcase challenge." You could only bring with you what fit into one suitcase. The day the team arrived in Bombay will forever be etched in my mind. Everything was different—sights, smells, people—it was surreal. There were people everywhere. I mean *everywhere*. I had never seen so many people in my life! I was overcome by the poverty. People were living in slums with no running water. Children were playing near streams where human waste floated by. These were people who never knew anything better. My mind could barely comprehend it all.

In first-world countries, we often live in a plastic bubble. We simply shut ourselves off from the plight of the poor. In India, at first I was scared, insecure and protective of myself. I was not at all like Jesus. Then later I became critical, harsh and annoyed— still not at all like Jesus! Yet, God was patient and merciful with me. I didn't deserve it. "Why wasn't I born in the slums of Bombay?" "Why didn't I have leprosy?" Only God knows, but the passage from James convicted me to the core. I decided to become grateful. I decided to help. I decided to have true faith!

As with any global problem (poverty, moral decay, abuse,

pollution, spiritual lostness, etc.) a difference can only be made one person at a time. I didn't pretend to think that I could solve all of India's poverty or health problems, but I was determined to make a difference any way I could. I knew that it was God's command to help the poor. "There will always be poor people in the land. Therefore I command you to be openhanded toward your brothers and toward the poor and needy in your land" (Deuteronomy 15:11).

I asked God for forgiveness and wisdom. He freely gave me the first and provided me the second by sending Dr. Merwin Richards (a new Indian disciple converted in San Francisco) and Dr. Yogaraj Guruswamy. The three of us came up with a plan and proposal to begin a one-of-a-kind mobile medical clinic that would serve the medical needs of the poor in Madras, India. I'm very grateful to HOPE *worldwide* and especially to Bob and Pat Gempel whose vision and love for the poor allowed this project to happen. The Madras Mobile Medical Clinic was one of the three original HOPE projects. Since 1990, thousands upon thousands of people have been given first-rate medical care free of charge, and many hundreds of lives have been saved. All this was because of a decision to make a difference (Proverbs 19:17).

I'm very thankful for the reminder the Indian leaders brought to my heart the day they toured my house. I don't want to have the heart of an "ugly American" who cares nothing for the plight of the poor. I want to have the heart of God (Jeremiah 22:16). Now I try to think, "Do I really need this?" before I buy something. We give thanks for the abundance that we have. Twice a year my children clean out their toy boxes and give their *best* toys to the orphanages in Tijuana, Mexico. My goal is for the San Diego church and the churches of the Southwest United States to be known as churches who not only love the lost, but who also love the poor. We have major HOPE projects in all of our churches, but there's much more to be done. So next time before you buy something, before you eat or before you turn on that garbage disposal, ask yourself these questions: "Do I love the poor?" "Am I making a difference with my life, my heart, my resources and with my time?" and "Do I truly have faith?"

10

Is There No Balm in Gilead?

MOE & AMANI BISHARA
Beruit, Lebanon

Elie is an orphan. He is skinny and dirty, and wears shabby clothes. His head is shaved. But he has sparkling eyes that captivate your heart and force you to hear his cry for love and attention.

The story is not new; you hear it over and over again. But how can we get used to seeing the pain of these kids? How can we be numb to their agony?! Elie is an eleven-year-old whom no one wants anymore. It's not his fault. He did nothing to deserve rejection. He falls asleep at night on the street wondering, *Where will I go? Who will accept me?* Imagine being born into a "family," then eleven years later they decide that you are not welcome anymore.

His real mother got pregnant while unmarried. During the war in Lebanon, not many could afford to get married, and Lebanon is a conservative Middle Eastern country where women could be killed for having a child out of wedlock. She gave him up for adoption to a family who, after a year, *sold him* to a rich family. They needed a son to keep their wealth in the family, according to the law. Not long afterward, the law was changed; they did not need or want him anymore and gave him up— rejection for the third time.

We will spare you the rest of the details of this child's misery, but today who is going to be his advocate? We could not just feel bad for him and then go home without doing anything to help. His silent cry was so loud, piercing our heart as it begged, "Help me."

Sin City in Shambles

Destruction, death, poverty and loss of everything—a few words that describe Lebanon after seventeen years of a cruel civil war. This is the new reality in Lebanon, and many find it

54

very hard to accept. In the recent past Lebanon was called "the Sodom and Gomorrah of the Middle East," "sin city," where everything was permissible. People have become embittered. Before the war they had the means to enjoy the temporary pleasures of sin; yet now, after losing everything, they can only lust after them. Pride prevents people from admitting their need for help. Instead, they decide to maintain the facade of the Mercedes cars and the French clothes no matter the cost—even if it means their own souls. A lot of men left the country to chase after their dreams of worldly success, leaving behind their wives and children with very little resources on which to survive. This has led many of these kids to turn into street children...begging, selling candy and forcing themselves on people, hoping to earn few pennies that will not even buy them a loaf of bread.

Lebanon is full of contradictions: It legalizes prostitution, yet condemns a little boy like Elie for being born to parents who could not afford to marry. It is a society that cares little about keeping the "inside" clean and much about keeping the "outside" clean. Prostitution is on the rise, and with it, the rapid increase of AIDS. Even during the heat of the war, brothels were protected by the most strict of the fundamentalist religious groups in Lebanon, for no one dared risk losing the large amounts of money they generated.

The Cry of My People

> O my Comforter in sorrow,
> my heart is faint within me.
> Listen to the cry of my people
> from a land far away:
> "Is the LORD not in Zion?
> Is her King no longer there?"
>
> Since my people are crushed, I am crushed;
> I mourn, and horror grips me.
> Is there no balm in Gilead?
> Is there no physician there?
> Why then is there no healing
> for the wound of my people?
> (Jeremiah 8:18-19a, 21-22).

Did the war bring about the sin that is so rampant in Lebanon? Certainly it had something to do with the new makeup of the society, but all the problems come from the same age-old root—the heart of man. When I (Mo) look at my people, I can not help but feel the pain Jeremiah felt when he heard the cry of his people: "Since my people are crushed, I am crushed...." I echo the same questions he asked, "Is there no balm in Gilead? Is there no physician there?" Street children, prostitution, orphans, poverty and disease—you see it all in the streets of our city.

What is the answer? It is not in stopping the war, reforming the economic situation, or providing a better political system. Certainly all these would be good things; they just are not enough in themselves. A child needs someone to care for him; a woman needs someone to love her for who she is and not for her body; the old man begging in the street needs a helping hand. In fact, all of us need love, acceptance and help. When we are adopted by God, he meets the most basic of these needs. He loves us and protects us; he shelters and makes us rich with every blessing in heaven and on earth. The least we can do is to seek to meet the needs of those who desperately need our help. Out of gratitude to God, we should be like that good Samaritan, who instead of just feeling bad and walking away, decided to do something about the hurting man's situation. God is calling on all of us to give of ourselves and to essentially give of what we have been given.

This child could be yours; that young woman could be your sister, and that begging old man your dad. Could you bear this thought? HOPE *worldwide* has provided true hope in Lebanon. With the help of God and many others we have been able to provide for several hundred sick children and to teach a few orphans, yet so much still needs to be done. The needs seem overwhelming, but with the power of God and with the prayers and initiative of disciples, we are confident that the job will be done.

It is time to look a needy person in the eyes and reassure him, "I am here for you. I will accept you and do whatever it takes to meet your needs." The question today has not changed much from the one Jeremiah asked many centuries ago: "Is there no physician there? Why then is there no healing?" Who will care for the slain of my people? Are you going to care?

Orphans

11

The Gift of Giving

RANDY & KAY MCKEAN
Boston, U.S.A.

Their smiles greet us each day as we walk through the kitchen. Suevonne, Walter and Krisstopher's photo on our refrigerator cheerfully reminds us of the birth of a family. We knew Suevonne as a vivacious single woman, and Walter as an outgoing and friendly single man. We watched as they found one another and fell in love, and we witnessed the marriage ceremony that brought them together as husband and wife. We waited with them as they yearned to adopt a child. Like with many young couples, however, the financial implications of adoption seemed daunting. But Suevonne and Walter had God on their side...and the love and support of many Christian friends. Disciples in the Boston area had been regularly contributing money that would benefit prospective adoptive couples. With the help of these funds, Suevonne and Walter were able to take little Krisstopher into their home as their own son.

Anyone who watched the adoption ceremony will remember Walter, with tears streaming down his cheeks, lifting his infant son high into the air for all to see. We all felt their joy, but we also felt the joy that comes with giving. Each of us who had contributed to the "adoption fund" felt that we were not just spectators, but were truly sharing in a precious event. By the grace of God, we had been enabled to give.

> And now, brothers, we want you to know about the grace that God has given the Macedonian churches. Out of the most severe trial, their overflowing joy and their extreme poverty welled up in rich generosity...they gave as much as they were able, and even beyond their ability...But just as you excel in everything—in faith, in speech, in knowledge, in complete earnestness and in your love for us—see that you also excel in this grace of giving (2 Corinthians 8:1-3, 7).

58

The apostle Paul's letter to the Corinthians includes a glowing report about a group of Christians in Macedonia. These disciples had undergone severe trials and extreme poverty, yet they had actually pleaded with Paul to be *allowed* to have the *privilege* of contributing to the needs of the saints! We can only imagine the conversation Paul might have had with the Macedonians concerning their desire to give:

> *"Please, Paul, we really would like to contribute to the saints who need some help!"*
>
> *"But you Macedonians have gone through so many trials..."*
>
> *"Well, this is true, we have had some severe trials as of late. But, as you know, other disciples around the world have gone through trials also, haven't they?"*
>
> *"Hmmm. Yes, I suppose you're right. No offense or anything, but you Macedonians are rather poor yourselves. How can you give anything to help others? Shouldn't you keep what you have?"*
>
> *"It's true we don't have much, but what we have we want to share!"*
>
> *"Well, I'm not sure if you should..."*
>
> *"Please, Paul, allow us the privilege of giving what we have..."*
>
> *"Why? Why do you so much want to give?"*
>
> *"Why? You want to know why? Look at what Jesus gave for us! He became poor for us, and now we feel so rich!"*

The Macedonians understood very clearly what, unfortunately, many disciples forget from time to time: To be able to give is a gift from God. It is a privilege to be able to give of our financial resources to help others. In addition to the obvious benefits of the ones in need, the act of opening up our hearts and our wallets is an act that God will use to bless *our* lives. This principle was often on Paul's heart throughout his ministry; we know he reminded the Ephesian elders that "it is more blessed to give than to receive" (Acts 20:35). The concept is one that might cause us to nod our heads in agreement, but it is important to remember why giving is good for us. The next time you are tempted to begrudge giving to those in need, remember these truths:

1. *Giving causes you to rely on God in faith and trust.* When we are strapped financially, the last thing that really makes sense to us is to give money away. We can easily bring to mind all the little projects and items that money could be used for in our own lives. When we give, we are admitting to God that we rely on him to meet all our needs and are willing to step out in faith. A step of faith is always pleasing to God.

2. *Giving draws you closer to the ones to whom you give.* Giving of yourself in any way to another has a remarkable way of drawing everyone involved closer. There is a bonding that occurs in being able to help someone, whether that person is nearby, as in the situation with Suevonne and Walter, or far away, as in the case of an orphan in Romania, a leper in India or an AIDS victim in Africa. Giving keeps these people in our prayers and on our hearts. We feel a kinship with them because in a small way we have had an influence on their lives.

3. *Giving allows us to become more like Jesus.* Jesus' whole purpose on this earth was to give his life for others. Throughout his ministry, he showed countless examples of considering the needs of others and helping them in any and every way. His death on the cross was the culmination of the selfless act of giving. It is this inspiring example that causes us to stop saying "What about *me*; what about *my* needs?" and to start saying, "I'm going to help someone else." When we give, even in small, meager ways, a little bit more of "self" dies and a little bit more of Jesus blossoms within us. We must never underestimate what a wonderful phenomenon it is to become more like Jesus!

These aspects of giving were probably what spurred on the disciples in Macedonia. Their generosity inspired Paul and so many others to contribute in order to help the poor. Today, we have numerous opportunities to help the poor by giving of our money, but it must not stop there. Our life motto must become: Give! Give our time! Give our energy! Give any resource we have! And when we give, we must also bow our heads and say, "Thank you, God, for the opportunity to grow in my trust. Thank you that I will draw closer to those I am giving to. Thank you that I can become more like my Lord Jesus. Thank you for the gift of being able to give."

12
God Loves the Alien

SCOTT & LYNNE GREEN
Hong Kong, China

The Chinese lifeguard was squinting and grinning at the riddle: one white male, one white female, one Chinese female, one white child and one Chinese child, all winging a Frisbee up and down the blazing beach to one another, all hugging one another with obvious affection. He wanted to ask but didn't dare: a Westerner with two wives, two families? Finally, gratefully, an alternative formed. "I get it!" he exclaimed to us. "This [Chinese] woman is your wife, and the Chinese girl your daughter; the white woman is your sister, and the boy is your nephew! Of course!"

The truth was much simpler: one Green family and one Chinese friend of the family. The Chinese girl is our adopted daughter, Ariel.

Typical thinking about typical families is, well, typical of the way man and God see things differently. Man sees adoption as unusual; God sees adoption as natural. Man fears that adopted children come with a flawed script; God showcases adopted children who lived a hero's script: Moses, Esther, Samuel (handed over to Eli), and Jesus (adopted by Joseph as his own). Man wonders who would be willing to take up the responsibility; God wonders who wouldn't? Now, after nearly six years with Ariel, we wonder why we didn't think of it sooner.

But there is so much more to learn from adoption than merely the call to adopt. Adoption *is* the story of the Bible: that God would trade his only Son in order to adopt us as sons. In fact, the adoption experience precisely parallels how God knows man and how he knows you. From Ariel, we understand God—his hopes, his dreams, his work, his strong, strong love—so much better. Most of all, we have come to understand that God loves the alien and that the alien is you and I!

Before adopting, we wrestled intermittently for many months with a common fear—that we would be somehow unable to bond with an adopted child in the same way we do with children born of our own flesh: *Will I feel the same about him? Will I be able to feel the same love for her?* Our first day with Ariel at the orphanage brought this issue into dazzling focus. Suddenly, the gravity of our differences with her flattened us: We didn't look alike, we didn't speak the same language, and we had no nine month pregnancy period to serve as a foundation for the relationship. Boom, here she was!

And this is how God experiences his relationship with every single one of us. Let's not confuse God's vision—"Let us make man in our image" (Genesis 1:26)—with God's mission: "There is no one righteous, not even one…no one who seeks God" (Romans 3:10-11). We have been, according to Scripture, totally *unlike* God! We have been "enemies" and "alienated" (Colossians 1:21). *Aliens!* We have been less attractive than any orphan on the planet! And God could have run. He could have hesitated. He could have despaired. Yet, because he "calls things that are not as though they were" (Romans 4:17), God chose to adopt us: "So you are no longer a slave but a son; and since you are a son, God has also made you an heir." We have been rescued, in fact, from an orphanage called "Darkness."

How do we respond to this utterly unlikely inheritance? With an evangelism worthy of the adoption experience:

> He defends the cause of the fatherless and the widow, and loves the alien, giving him food and clothing. And you are to love those who are aliens, for you yourselves were aliens in Egypt (Deuteronomy 10:18-19).

If God can love aliens, then we can love the alienated. If God can relate to us, then we can relate to anybody. If God, through Jesus, became like us, then we can and *must* become all things to all men. If God sees sons in the place of slaves, then we can see future brothers and sisters instead of "non-Christians"!

It is an ongoing joke in the China Sector that Scott and Lynne are honorary Teo Chiu-nese (we like the food), but there is some truth to it. We have learned the language. We have adapted to the food (gratefully—it's the world's best), the culture and the unusual limitations of living in the world's most crowded city. We have immersed ourselves in Chinese geography and history. It is hard, but it is powerful. God used this learning process to convert and raise up amazing native leaders for the China Sector and to enrich and mature us personally. In the same way, when you are willing to speak a non-Christian's emotional language, when you are willing to understand him, when you are willing to walk miles in his shoes, even as you try to refit him with better boots, he will feel the awesome power of the adoptive heart of God, working through you.

And his gratitude and response, multiplied over many lives and years, will most certainly sound like the delight that soars in Ariel's sweet laugh.

DOUGLAS & JOYCE ARTHUR
Washington, D.C., U.S.A.

Children Are for Loving

We had the perfect family: one boy, one girl, one year apart. Adoption wasn't for us. Maybe it would be if we only had boys or only had girls or couldn't have any at all. We were set. We needed to preach about adoption, but we didn't need to do it.

We were inspired when the Greens adopted, but not convicted. You see, we had the perfect family. It was Joyce who was the first to crack: She began to think maybe it wasn't a question of what we *needed* as much as it was what we could *give*. Why not share our perfect family with someone who had none at all? Wasn't there enough love to go around? Was our house really too small and our car not roomy enough? Verses like "Anyone, then, who knows the good he ought to do and doesn't do it sins" (James 4:17) began to take on a new meaning. The issue began to change from the "principle" of adoption to the "people" who needed to be adopted.

Not long after that, the Gempels returned home from their first visit to the Shanghai orphanage with a video of the children. We watched those small children sing a song about being little flowers that would blossom one day, and the tears began to flow. We were gone...lost in a total wave of compassion for people who had nobody at all.

'Principles' Are for Debating—'People' Are for Loving

Then we made a big "mistake," one that would cost us thousands of dollars (nearly enough for a new car) and hundreds of hours in the next several months: We took a trip to see orphans in Shanghai and New Delhi. All hope of ever being "logical" and discussing the "principle" of adoption was destroyed. It changes you when you hold a child who has never seen you before but looks at you like children look at Santa Claus—with joy, fascination and expectation. It changes you when little girls smile just to be held by somebody, anybody, because they have nobody at all. It was a mistake all right, that is, if we wanted to "protect" our perfect family.

After returning home, our decision was emotional and irrevocable: Our perfect family was about to improve. We decided since our children would be ten and eleven years old, we wanted a little girl between two and four years old. Two months later the call came from India: "We have your child."

We leapt for joy. "How old is she?"

"He is eight years old came the reply."

"There must be some mistake—we are the four-year-old-girl family." The nuns response was classic: "I know your family, and trust me, this boy is for you. I have prayed about it, and in twenty years in this business I have never been wrong!"

We were amazed at her confidence and her batting average, but we still asked, "Can we meet him?"

"No! He's had enough rejection already. But I will send a picture." Within days the package arrived with the picture and description of Ajit. He'd had a hard life: He had lived on the street for five years, and he had several scars to show for it. But he had a great smile.

Later that day we were back on the phone to India. Joyce had the final question: What does Ajit think about being adopted? Through the static of a bad connection came a crystal clear response: "Every night he takes the older kids in the orphanage upstairs where they kneel in a circle, and he leads them in a prayer that they can all find families one day." The tears rolled down Joyce's face...decision made, life saved. You see "principles" are for debating—"people" are for loving.

Last week we celebrated our first anniversary with Nathanael "Ajit" Arthur. We had Indian food and shared our favorite memories. We're much closer as a family now. We all speak English. Christopher and Nathanael both claim the other is their best friend, and Jessica loves having a "little" brother (even if he is an inch taller than she).

We were amused to hear recently that Marty and Chris Fuqua, friends of ours and church leaders over a sizable ministry, had also made a costly "mistake." They too had a perfect family. Ben and Maria are great kids. Marty, a former collegiate wrestler, is more known for "grit" than "gooey sentimentality." He, like so many, thought the principle of adoption was great for someone else. Last summer he was spending time in Moscow, helping the ministry and an orphanage, when he met "Anya," a nine-year-old girl with no family and a warm heart. Lord willing, Anya will be a Fuqua early next year.

The Fuquas, like we, learned that "principles" are for debating—"people" are for loving.

13

Does Anyone
Care That I Was Born?

JEANIE SHAW
Boston, U.S.A.

Bucharest, Romania: A city that has changed my perspective and changed my heart. My mind is filled with images from previous trips there. The scenes flash by...We are at the train station. From out of nowhere gather what seems to be a crowd of street children, begging for something, anything, that I have. The children at the hospital are also engraved on my mind's eye. I still can see the little orphan boy dying right before my eyes, with no one to hold his hand or reassure him. I remember my lunch at the new McDonald's restaurant: To this city it is somewhere special. While we were eating lunch, a bride and groom and their wedding party, in full wedding attire, came through the doors to enjoy their wedding feast.

My favorite place in Bucharest is a little building tucked away from easy view. It is one of the many Houses of Children that are home to the nearly 200,000 orphans of this country— Casa de Copii Nr. 4. Here live about a hundred children. They are between three and twelve years old. They come in all shapes and sizes, yet have one thing in common: They want to be loved. They want someone to care that they were born.

As I write this I am on a plane, headed back to my comfortable home and loving family—a contrast to what these children have and know. Yesterday at the orphanage I went to a birthday party. We played games, sang, blew out candles on a cake and opened presents. The children love it when it is their turn for the birthday party. What a wonderful sight to see disciples from the church in Bucharest playing with the children, giving them love and individual attention. Their little faces brighten with smiles, and hugs come freely when they see these friendly faces. Even though the children often do not know when they were born, these HOPE volunteers know. Volunteers also know in Boston, where each child has a sponsor family who picks out their birthday present and lovingly sends it to be shipped across the sea.

Each time I come to Romania I take home with me cherished memories of the children and deepened convictions. Convictions to truly care that the individuals I meet were born and to let them feel that care. The poor and needy need me to care. The truth is, *I need them.* They cause me to examine my heart and deepen my convictions.

I need to be reminded day after day to be grateful. Why did I grow up with loving parents in a free country? It is nothing I deserve—only a gift from God. I am grateful, yet I know my gratitude is only shown by what I do with what I have been given. Every time I see people in need, I have the choice to be selfish, as if I deserved what I've been given, or selfless. How grateful are you?

Working with those in need teaches me to love people from the heart. It is one thing to see a mass of little bodies and work with them as they hang on us and won't let go. Some smell bad and most have runny noses. Yet, it is another when one of those children climbs up on my knee, clasps my hand with one small hand, strokes my hair with another, and looks up at me and says, "Mama." The tears stream down and my heart breaks again. Without touching them up close, my "good deeds" can become merely a job and a duty. I need this touch to teach me to love as Jesus did as he reached out and touched those around him. How up-close and personal is your giving?

I also need the poor and needy in my life to teach me more about the love of God. I have learned so much about God's love from a little orphan boy named Iacob. Iacob has never been visited by a mother or a father. He has no family, shares a room with about twenty other boys and is not even sure how old he is. About a year ago Iacob's eyes caught mine. They sparkled. He smiled at me and followed me around. He sought out a relationship with me.

Soon Iacob will be our son. He will have a family who loves him deeply. I already have his suitcase packed. It has his brother's hand-me-downs and some brand new clothes bought just for him. His sisters and I carefully searched for just the right outfit for his trip home. We measured him to make sure his clothes would fit "just right." Yesterday we put a New England Patriots cap on his head to his deep approval. He walked around as if he were king. We talked of his coming to America, having a family, a new life, a new language. Our entire family waits with eagerness to lavish our love on him.

Then it hit me. Ephesians 1:3-6 took on deeper meaning:

> Praise be to the God and Father of our Lord Jesus Christ, who has blessed us in the heavenly realm with every spiritual blessing in Christ. For he chose us in him before the creation of the world to be holy and blameless in his sight. In love he predestined us to be adopted as his sons through Jesus Christ, in accordance with his pleasure and will—to the praise of his glorious grace, which he has freely given us in the One he loves.

God has had my suitcase packed for a long time. He's carefully measured me, wanting to make sure the contents fit "just right." So many of its contents I already enjoy: my relationship with him, my marriage, my children, my friends. It is nearly unfathomable to me that God could love me like that. I am so grateful for what Iacob has taught me about God's love. Do you delight in the knowledge that God has your own suitcase packed?

The poor and needy desperately need our love and touch. This is clear. I believe we have just as deep a need to love and touch the poor and needy.

I close with a question that was asked by one of Iacob's friends. He visited the church in Bucharest with Iacob, turned to my friend Aileen and said, "I heard Iacob found a mommy. Is that because he is so well behaved? What do I need to do to find a mommy?" The question is not what *he* needs to do. The question is what do *we* need to do?

Do you care that they were born? What will you do to make their dreams come true?

14

Something More for the Orphans of China

DAN & ELEXA LIU
Hong Kong

There are hundreds, thousands, perhaps even more orphans in China. Through HOPE *worldwide*, we have had the privilege to visit a handful of China's orphanages and to work in one closely for some time. It was there that we were able to bond with not just numbers or statistics but with real children.

Touched by a Human

Every day for a month we went up to the second floor where the infants and toddlers lived. The children were contained in row after row of cribs. Most of us didn't know the first thing about child development from a medical or psychological stand-point, but we did know that the children needed to get out of their cribs, out of their layers and layers of clothing and onto the mats so that they could crawl, explore and play.

I (Dan) felt very humbled working with the children. They had no parents, and there were so many of them that often I felt inadequate. All that I managed to do was play with them, be their friend for awhile and then leave for the day. I remember one little girl, about a year and a half old, whom I helped give massage therapy to. Most of the children had some muscle atrophy from the lack of exercise and in addition, this girl had a form of epilepsy. Whenever I saw her, she was always lying in her crib very quiet and still.

At first, when I gently massaged her feet and the calves of her legs, she seemed startled; but then she started to relax. After only a short time, a smile appeared on her face and she began to make a gentle cooing sound. After I finished one leg, she gingerly held up the other leg for me to massage. It really hit me then that no one had ever treated her with as much love and tenderness as this. I saw that what little I could do *was* making a difference.

We all became very attached to the kids. We fed them, made toys for them and sometimes simply held them in our arms. One volunteer named a special little girl "Sunshine" because of the joy that the girl gave her. My little friend bore an amazing resemblance to our own son, Brian, so we named her Briana. The orphanage caregivers began to notice the resemblance and joked around telling Briana to call me "Papa" whenever I came into the room. After a week or two she became so comfortable with me that she called me that.

Real Religion

As I write this article, I feel a sense of incompleteness. We haven't seen Briana for over a year now. For various reasons we were unable to continue working with the children there. We don't know how she is doing or how her life will turn out. But I know one reason why God allowed me to meet her—so I would be as determined as ever to serve the orphans, to serve the "Brianas" of China, so more and more could find love and find homes.

> Religion that God our Father accepts as pure and faultless is this: to look after orphans and widows in their distress and to keep oneself from being polluted by the world (James 1:27).

The Bible says that we need to look after orphans "in their distress." This is acceptable religion. We should note that the passage preceding this verse convicts us with this command: "Do not merely listen to the word, and so deceive yourselves. Do what it says" (James 1:22). Plain and simple, each one of us needs to obey the Scriptures and look after orphans in whatever way we can. It is not enough to simply be moved emotionally by the stories we hear. Four years ago helping the orphans in China was just a dream that Bob and Pat Gempel and Scott and Lynne Green had. But it didn't remain a dream. Their hearts brought together a simple challenge: Just do something. And so we did.

In early 1994 HOPE *worldwide* organized a nationwide medical seminar on children's rehabilitation in China. Doctors, teachers and orphanage directors from all over China attended. Shortly thereafter, we helped open a channel for American families who wanted to adopt. Chinese orphans are now in loving homes. These orphans' lives have totally changed.

Today, the charge is to "Just do something *more*." HOPE is already planning its second nationwide medical seminar to train Chinese orphanage medical personnel. Every bit makes a difference. With orphans, just giving a little means a great deal. A tender touch brings joy. What most of the orphans in China need right now are simply acts of love that will help them to grow and develop. That's what happened two years ago and enabled these children, many of whom were considered unadoptable, to be adopted into Christian homes.

So, just go and do something more for the orphans. Raise money or donate your own money so that we can continue to do more together. Do outreach at an orphanage, or become a foster parent. Raise funds for a family who is planning to adopt, or decide to adopt yourself. When we all just do something more, then many orphans' lives will be transformed, and we will all be more like our God.

15
Shining Stars

SHAWN & LENA WOOTEN
Moscow, Russia

The stage is set. The music is playing. The television cameras are rolling. Thousands are applauding and cheering. On stage the performers captivate the audience with their energetic dance. Focused, they do not even flinch with one of the world's most famous entertainers in the audience. Who are these talented young artists? More than 700 orphans from twenty-four different orphanages in Moscow, Russia. This is the first annual HOPE *worldwide* Sports Festival, designed to bring the extraordinary to children who often see less than the ordinary.

The Parent-less Trap

With the overwhelming problems in Russia, there is little time for anyone to think of planning celebrations for these children. The sheer number of orphans is staggering. There are 700,000 children in orphanages and thousands more in the streets. The people in Moscow don't really talk about the orphans unless it is some new horror story about stolen bikes or broken windows or a twelve-year-old becoming pregnant. Most discussions end with comments like, "Nothing good will come of them anyway." The orphans know that these attitudes exist. They feel the separation that comes when neighborhood parents won't allow their own children to mix with them. The orphans' basic needs are met, but little is done to show the children that they are special.

The HOPE Festival was a chance for these children to celebrate the fact that they *are* special. As the children entered the hall, volunteers from the Moscow Church of Christ rose to their feet and applauded these children who have endured tragic circumstances. All 2,700 children who attended the event went home with different prizes and gifts, a vision that life can be spectacular, and most importantly, the feeling that they are special. HOPE *worldwide* in Moscow is working hard to continue making the children's lives special by other events, including birthday parties for the children. Through these ongoing relationships we are hoping to change the current statistics that predict 30 percent of orphans will become vagrants, 20 percent will be jailed and 10 percent will commit suicide.

> "He defended the cause of the poor and the needy,
>   and so all went well.
> Is that not what it means to know me?"
>   declares the Lord (Jeremiah 22:16).

Since my wife and I started to work with orphans, we have seen our lives change. I remember the first orphanage in Kiev, Ukraine, that we visited. I kept some distance from the children in my heart because I was afraid that if I got too close, I would feel how they feel. Their world scared me: to know that no one is left in the world to care for me; to know that I am someone's responsibility, not their joy; and to know that if I were to die, I would die alone with no one to miss me.

Sick and Alone

Natasha, a young girl from Orphanage 15 woke up at 2:00 A.M. in her bed with a high temperature. Afraid and alone, she was put in an ambulance and taken to a hospital. She felt so sick that she was afraid she wasn't going to make it back to the orphanage—the only home she really knew. Who will lose sleep over the fact that she is sick? So many nights Natasha had cried herself to sleep because her only dream is to have a mom and dad. Did it really matter to anyone if she made it back? It would be one less mouth to feed, one less future criminal, one less problem. When HOPE volunteers came on Saturday to the orphanage, I realized that Natasha was not at the orphanage. I asked around and the other children said she was sent to the hospital. When I asked, "When?" They answered, "Thursday," and immediately

I got this gut-wrenching feeling in my stomach. For two days this child was sick and all alone.

After several calls by the administration we finally found out which hospital she was in. The next morning at 6:00 A.M. I got up early so I could visit her. I couldn't stand the idea that a child that God loves so much could go another day without knowing that someone loves her. Natasha was in a room with four other girls. The others all had parents who visited two or three times a day. Natasha lay alone and without hope.

We arrived at the hospital at 8:00 A.M. When told she had some visitors, she came out of her room not able to even guess who had come. She was so grateful to see us. We played some games, and I gave her some fruits and the *Lion King* book. I asked her if she was surprised to see me, and she told me she thought it was a mistake when the doctor told her.

As we left the hospital, we looked up at her window and there she was with the other four girls. Now she was like the others. Someone loved her. Someone cared for her. As she waved good-bye from the window, I saw a huge smile on her face, and I knew she felt God's grace: Someone loves me who doesn't have to; someone sacrificed for me who didn't have to.

That someone is Jesus. I understood in that moment I was once an orphan just like Natasha. I carried that same fear in my heart of being alone every day, until God found me and brought me into his family. Without God we are all orphans. It is HOPE's ambition, as it is God's, for us to love the orphans like our own children. What does it mean to be like God? What does it mean to be like Christ? Is it not to defend the cause of the poor and needy? How much are you being like Christ today? Every orphan needs someone in their life to remind them that they are loved. Through our examples these children will see and know they have a heavenly Father.

Troubled Cities

16

Filled with Compassion

MARK TEMPLER
London, England

It was the spring of 1995. Our three-year-olds, Luke and Esther, were playing exuberantly in the back porch of our New Delhi flat. Suddenly they threw a little red toy cup over the high back wall. They said, "Daddy, Daddy, please get it!" So I climbed up and leaned over the edge, looking into the alley behind our house. There among the rubbish was the red cup. A little girl clothed in rags was in the alley, and I called out to her, asking her to throw the cup up to me. But she ran away. So I climbed down and told the kids that we'd have to get it ourselves.

We walked outside and entered the alley. But the cup was gone! Luke and Esther were distraught. We began looking for it, and I noticed that there was a small hut in the side of the alleyway, about twenty meters from our house. A vegetable-seller lived there with his family. I spoke to him, and asked about the cup and the girl who played in the alley. He said the girl was his daughter. Then he uncovered his vegetable cart, and there was the cup! I could see the little girl hiding behind his hut (only three-feet high, six-feet long and four-feet wide).

At that moment I realized that these people were my neighbors. They lived just a few meters from my home, and *I had not noticed them in the two years I lived there.* Ramprasad had lived there for about ten years with his wife, Shanthi Devi, his 8-year-old son Aashish, and his seven-year-old daughter Seema. They had no toilet, no electricity, no running water and no toys. Two of them had to sleep outside because the hut was so small. They survived on 1000 rupees per month ($30). At this point my selfishness and apathy convicted me. I was worried about a lost toy while there are people next door to me in pain...people I don't even know! How easily my heart can harden to the needs of people as I justify myself by thinking, "I do a lot for the poor."

Taking It Home

We went home and talked about their family. When we returned with ten toys, it was like Seema and Aashish's very first Christmas. We invited Ramprasad's family to church, but they politely declined, explaining that they were too busy working. Tears came to our eyes at family devotional that evening as Nadine and I spoke to Luke and Esther about this family's day-to-day life. We thought about what it would be like to trade places with them. Just a short time earlier we had been so concerned about one lost toy. These two children had never even had one toy to lose. And these were our neighbors!

In the following weeks, we had the chance to meet another poor family, this one 200 meters from our house. Bijender, who is crippled and made his living as a tea-seller, had lived there twenty years with his wife and three kids. We gave his kids toys, and started regularly giving his family our leftover food. They were so grateful. They came and ate with us in our home. Bijender even came to church one time, and studied the Bible with us! Every time our kids passed Ramprasad or Bijender's huts, they could see their children playing with the toys we had given. They experienced a feeling no amount of money could buy.

The Compassion of Jesus

A man with leprosy came to him and begged him on his knees, "If you are willing, you can make me clean."

Filled with compassion, Jesus reached out his hand and touched the man. "I am willing," he said. "Be clean!" Immediately the leprosy left him and he was cured (Mark 1:40-42).

Jesus was willing to go out of his way to reach out to the hurting and to touch their lives. He was not so wrapped up in his own life, his own cares, his own worries that he could not see the needs of others. He reached out and touched the untouchable. Caring about the poor, people in need, or our neighbors, is a simple choice: Do we pay attention, or do we look the other way, afraid of what we might see? We don't need to travel to the third world to see poverty and suffering. We just need to open our eyes. Jesus met needs as he saw them. He mingled among the people and embraced them in their suffering. He listened to people's problems and did his best to help them.

As Jesus told the parable of the good Samaritan, he taught us to embrace those we encounter as our neighbors. The Samaritan did. He gave his time, his money and a commitment to follow up with the innkeeper (Luke 10:25-37).

Open Your Eyes

Today, what is *your* lost toy? Bills? Broken things? Holidays? Investments? Other people in our own cities, near to us, are in great need. They need help doing something they can't do themselves. They need a friend to listen to them, someone to call them, someone to care. In Haggai 1:4, the prophet challenged the people: "Is it a time for you yourselves to be living in your paneled houses, while this house remains a ruin?" Our materialism can make us neglect the house of God. But the house of God is no rich man's house, where the poor are outside, begging at the gate (Luke 16:19-21). God's house is where the poor, the crippled, the lame and the blind are invited and welcomed in (Luke 14:13-14).

Brothers and sisters, let us have compassion on people around us. In our neighborhoods, workplaces and even our churches, there are people who are hard to love and in great need. Do you really care for them? Or do you just care for those who are similar to you, easier to relate to? Do you make the opportunity to find people in need, or do you stick to a comfortable routine?

Helping the poor is not just about participating in programs and giving money, though these things are great. It is an attitude of the heart that starts with caring about people around us. When we forget about our lost toys and soften our hearts, God will bless us with a joy the world can never take away!

17

How Deserted Lies the City

Douglas & Joanne Webber
Los Angeles, U.S.A.

Riots! Fires! Gunshots! Gangs! Drugs! Drive-bys! Robberies! Car jackings! Home invasions! Muggings! Rapes! Kidnappings! Homelessness! Murders! Don't go near that neighborhood at night! Make sure you lock your doors! Don't forget to turn on the alarm! Watch your car! Watch your purse! Watch your kids! HELP!!!

Do you feel scared being in the city? Do you want to raise your kids there? Do you want to live there? Does anyone want to be there?

It is no secret to anyone who spends time in America's inner cities that the problems seem as insurmountable as ever. It has now been more than twenty-five years since the National Advisory Commission on Civil Disorders, commenting on the urban riots of the 1960s, stated that "our nation is moving toward two societies, one black, one white—separate and unequal." Over that time, changes such as federal programs of employment training, educational subsidies, housing assistance and welfare reforms have been enacted. Yet despite these and other "institutional" reforms, the human tragedies of drugs, gangs, violence, unemployment, broken families, HIV/AIDS, teen pregnancy, failed schools, despair and alienation are more prevalent than ever in the inner cities of America. However, in order to begin affecting behavior, we must begin to understand not only the scope of the problem, but its root as well.

What is needed is not a halting but a reversing of these negative trends. While expenditures on elementary and secondary education have increased more than 200 percent since 1960, SAT scores have declined 73 points. Since 1960, while the U.S. population has increased by only 41 percent, the number of violent crimes has increased more than 550 percent! In 1943 in

New York City, there were 44 homicides by gunshot and in 1991 there were 1,499. In 1991, in ten major cities (Detroit, Washington D.C., St. Louis, Newark, Atlanta, Cleveland, Baltimore, Philadelphia, Chicago and Pittsburgh), more than 50 percent of all births were out of wedlock.

It must be noted that many of these problems are not limited to the poor, nonwhite communities of America. In the 1992 book *The Day America Told the Truth*, in comparing predominantly white Beverly Hills (limousines, mansions and an average family income in excess of $100,000) with the mostly Hispanic and black South Bronx (many half-abandoned, gutted tenements and an average family income of less than $10,000), the authors had some "surprising" findings. Though child abuse is sadly very common in the South Bronx, it occurs no less in Beverly Hills. People in Beverly Hills are much more likely to commit adultery, twice as likely to use illegal drugs, twice as likely to have committed a crime themselves, and twice as likely to have shot someone with a handgun than people living in the South Bronx! The authors additionally found a third more people living in Beverly Hills than in the South Bronx to have considered suicide.

These and similar statistics from other communities strike at the opinions of many that primarily economic factors lie behind the behavioral patterns prevalent in the inner cities of America. That basic position would suggest that these problems can be cured from without by more good jobs at good wages and by changing government policy to provide less welfare, thereby underwriting less irresponsible behavior.

Being Part of the Solution

How deserted lies the city,
    once so full of people!
How like a widow is she,
    who once was great among the nations!
She who was a queen among the provinces
    has now become a slave.
Bitterly she weeps at night,
    tears are upon her cheeks.

Among all her lovers
    there is none to comfort her.
All her friends have betrayed her;
    they have become her enemies (Lamentations 1:1-2).

If progress is to be made, patterns of behavior that lead to low academic achievement, criminality, drug use, unwed childbearing and the like must change. We must teach people a whole new way to live. It becomes clear that the behavioral problems in our cities are rooted primarily in spiritual issues. A man's spiritual and moral convictions influence his understanding of parental and marital responsibilities, as well as his understanding of himself. How can sexual abstinence or the rejection of violence be taught effectively without a spiritual or moral appeal? It becomes clear that, as a society, over the past several decades we have suffered the consequences of selfishness, greed and last (but definitely not least), a lack of spiritual conviction and public discourse.

What can we do to make a difference in the cities of America? There can be no better example for anyone than Jesus Christ and his disciples. He preached to meet people's *spiritual* and *eternal* needs, and yet served on a daily basis to meet people's *physical* and *immediate* needs (Mark 1:32-39, 6:6b-12; Matthew 20:28, etc.). He calls everyone to follow his example and do the same. What is not needed are one-time-only acts of kindness or outspokenness by individuals. What is needed is a long-term commitment to causes dedicated to improving our communities. Also essential is the ongoing courage to make disciples of Jesus by being outspoken for moral and spiritual values.

Who will volunteer to chair a committee, serve on a board, commit to showing up at a given time one day a week to serve the elderly and sick, or to tutor underprivileged children? Who will volunteer to help restore and beautify public parks and buildings, or organize food and clothing drives for the homeless? There are many who would like to volunteer but will not take time away from their family to do so. There are many others who will not take the time away from themselves to do it.

Though we must strike a balance, it is important to remember that when we volunteer *with* our children, we will teach our children by example. We will teach our children to grow up into caring and compassionate adults with spiritual convictions. We will teach our children to consider others better than ourselves.

It is going to take courage, determination and selflessness to be caring and compassionate and to instill these qualities in our children and others. It is going to take a constant and continual commitment, expecting nothing in return. We can individually and collectively work to restore our cities. They are eagerly awaiting us!

18
Caring Takes Courage

BUD & KITTY CHILES
New York City, U.S.A.

November seventh was a typical Saturday for Ariel and his team of HOPE for Kids volunteers. But all that changed the instant bullets started to fly in a Newark tenement.

Ariel is a team leader whose responsibility is to coordinate volunteers working to help needy children get connected with healthcare providers. The Newark project is one of ten "missed immunization appointment" (MIA) projects in the New York region. Ariel was encouraged that particular morning because his fellow workers were literally fanning out all over the inner cities of New York and New Jersey. Although Ariel and his team worked regular jobs, they were excited to sacrifice their Saturday to find families in need. Educating families and working to get kids into their local clinics for immunization against deadly childhood diseases is very rewarding work. Ariel knew that HOPE for Kids had successfully worked over the last three years educating hundreds of thousands of families and immunizing tens of thousands of children across the country. He and his team were encouraged that the small project they had helped to start in Harlem in 1993 had mushroomed into HOPE for Kids with projects in sixty American cities involving 30,000 volunteers and reaching over one million children annually.

The mission that Saturday was very straightforward. Ariel was assigned 100 children from the local public health department that had failed to show up for their scheduled immunization appointments. Ariel carefully divided the thirty volunteers into teams that provided the most security for that specific area. Each volunteer would need to find three kids to complete the job. Ariel knew, however, that it was not that simple. He knew that they would find only one-third of their assigned kids at home. One-third would be out and the other third would have moved.

"That's why no other group but HOPE wants to do this job," he thought as they entered the first building. "Who else would persevere until they track down these families?"

Ariel was uncomfortable even before they got inside the projects. High-rise housing in Newark's inner city is a dangerous place for everyone, even for those who prey on the vulnerability of people trapped in this deadly system. He knew that God was watching out for his team, but the suspicious looks, broken glass, filth, blaring rap music and a bit of street knowledge shook his feelings of security. Ariel was on edge as they entered the crowded courtyard and saw eight teens gathered in a heated discussion. He was immediately conscious that the other three members of his team were two women and a two-year-old child. The youths did not welcome the group of strangers he was leading into their building. He was within twenty feet of the youths when he realized he had made a serious mistake. They were not just agitated; they were having a furious altercation. Shouts were followed by pushing and blows. Quickly, Ariel told the women to run. At the same moment, one of the youths split from the group and ran toward the women. The sound of gunfire exploded and the youth fell from a shot to his back. His body lay in the place where the women had been standing only seconds before.

A Close-up Look

Children are dying in the inner cities of America. It is a daily fact of life. Violence, poverty, disease and distress all take an immeasurable toll. Many of us, as disciples, are getting our first close look at what is and has been a fact all over the world—there are "those who have" and "those who have not." Those "who have not" experience real, everyday suffering in a way that "those who have" cannot begin to understand.

We can visit the garbage mountains in Manila, but we do not live there. We can see the photographs of the Rwandan refugees, but we do not feel their hunger pains day after day. We can read about the impact and spread of HIV/AIDS, but it is not destroying our own bodies. Across every continent, the poor and needy cry out silently for relief. Who will help? Who will come? Who will care?

The Scriptures say that God will help, God will come, God cares:

> For he will deliver the needy who cry out,
>   the afflicted who have no one to help.
> He will take pity on the weak and the needy
>   and save the needy from death.
> He will rescue them from oppression and violence,
>   for precious is their blood in his sight
>   (Psalm 72:12-14).

How will he care? How will he come? How will he help? Once he came through Jesus; through him he expressed his care and concern and brought help for the poor and needy. But Jesus promised that we would do greater things than he! In Mark 8:2, Jesus shows us how:

> A man with leprosy came to him and begged him on his knees, "If you are willing, you can make me clean."
> Filled with compassion, Jesus reached out his hand and touched the man. "I am willing," he said. "Be clean!"
> (Mark 1:40-41).

If we are willing, we can help the needy to be nourished, housed, healed and employed. Are you willing? Will you raise your hand when help is needed, or will you hold back? Remember, Jesus was willing.

Ariel and his team members were willing. They made sure that the police were notified that day. Then they finished finding the families on their list. In their hearts they grieved for the young man who had been gunned down. They might not have been as self-confident as they had been that morning, but they were God-confident. They knew that God had protected them. And they also knew the only way to provide real hope was to continue to "be willing" to care, to go and to help.

Our dream is that HOPE *worldwide* will soon represent the largest, most effective volunteer force the world has ever seen. Our dream is that your own committed and courageous heart will unite with tens of thousands of others around the world. With each selfless thought we think, each wound we bandage, each meal we serve, each door we knock, each prayer we utter, we are the hands of God to those in need. And as our light shines in the dark places, others will follow our example. As we care, so will they; as we go, so will they; as we help, so will they.

19
Setting the Captives Free

WALTER EVANS
Philadelphia, U.S.A.

Visualize yourself in a life-threatening situation, not knowing where to go, not having anyone to help. Seeing the building burning around you and yet, being exhausted from panic and wearied by fear, you simply sit down and let it happen.

Many of us take getting out of harm's way for granted. We know what we would do in an emergency. We teach our children how to dial 911 at the first sign of trouble. We have trained professionals all around us who will come to our rescue night or day.

This is not the case for men and women on the inner city streets of Philadelphia taken captive by fear and chemicals: No emergency exit plan exists, and no rescue team is waiting by the phone for their call. They sit on doorsteps feeling helpless as their lives crumble down around them. They can't see the way out.

That's where "the Rev" comes in. Founder of the nationally recognized "One Day at a Time" (ODAAT) program in Philadelphia, Henry Wells (the Rev) has been showing since 1983 that there is a way out of the chemical abuse trap of the inner city. The Rev has taken bold steps by fixing up houses throughout the inner city and building a community of people discarded by society. Because these individuals have hit absolute bottom with no other place to turn, they arrive at ODAAT ready to be interviewed and to be put through a "tough love" program that makes military boot camp seem like day care.

Seizing an Opportunity
The Spirit of the Sovereign LORD is on me,
because the LORD has anointed me
to preach good news to the poor.

He has sent me to bind up the brokenhearted,
to proclaim freedom for the captives
and release from darkness for the prisoners (Isaiah 61:1-2).

In 1991 when our leadership team arrived from the UK to work with the church in Philadelphia, at first we were taken aback by the enormity of the problems in the inner city. We wanted so much to begin a HOPE project in Philadelphia to provide some relief. Not knowing how to start or who to turn to, we began to ask around for help and input, and that's when we became acquainted with ODAAT.

Soon after our initial contact with ODAAT, the Rev invited Douglas Arthur and me to spend a day with the program. We witnessed an emotional entrance interview, had lunch in a former burned-out row house that had been fixed up. We went to "group" in the local community center. But the most impacting part of the day was spending time with the people. Douglas and I were surrounded by people who had found the escape hatch: homeless, drug addicts, HIV/AIDS sufferers, people the world had given up on. Even though ODAAT was tough on them in getting them to face their addictions, they embraced the challenge. They were finding solutions—they were beginning to see the light of freedom.

The leadership of the Greater Philadelphia Church of Christ (GPCC) decided to step in and help out. The spiritual side of ODAAT had been, for the most part, discarded. There was a tremendous need not only to break the addiction, but to build a spiritual foundation that the recovering addict could stand on. Yet we realized that we could not come in and teach the Gospel until these people had clear minds and open hearts. It was a time to wait, a time to pitch in and help ODAAT do its work.

Good medical care was the greatest need for the members of ODAAT and for the families of North Philadelphia. Throughout the area family health centers have been boarded up, abandoned and left in ruin. The GPCC took on the challenge and invested ten months of time, money and volunteer-help to build the HOPE Medical Clinic. Staffed by disciples, the clinic has caught the attention of the community and the city, not only for its excellent care, but also the love shown by the staff to the patients.

After the health clinic was up and running, more ODAAT needs became apparent. The building housing their rehabilitative and counseling program was about to be sold out from under them. The church held a special contribution and $45,000 was raised to buy the building back for ODAAT.

A tremendous rally was held on May 1, 1993, as the members of the GPCC joined hands with ODAAT for a "Clean-Up Philly Day." Officials from the city, the U.S. Congress and the community joined us. After an exciting day of hard work, all the members of the church and ODAAT joined together at the community center as the check for $45,000 was presented. There were many prayers of thanks and songs of joy as we all celebrated this great victory.

ODAAT is not the absolute solution, nor will it ever be. The only lasting solution is found in Christ. Yet "One Day at a Time" has shown that people can be set free from the captivity that enslaves them and be brought to a point where their hearts and minds can be open and receptive to the call of God. The members of the GPCC are grateful to men like Henry Wells who, by sheer courage and determination, have opened the doors that so many said could never be opened.

Happily Ever After

After many months of being around the church, the Rev began to study the Bible. He was first impressed by the Gempels' spiritual lives, then began studying the Bible with Douglas Arthur. Soon Henry Wells began to open up and come to terms with his own need for God, his own need to be set free. He and Chris Reed, the lead evangelist for the GPCC, became close friends, and after months of wrestling with the Scriptures and his past, the Rev made his decision. On January 4, 1996, Henry Wells was baptized into Christ during a celebration for HOPE! Henry Wells now knows the full joy of walking with his God one day at a time.

20

The Spirit Strikes in the Inner City

PHIL & DONNA LAMB
Miami, U.S.A.

When people think of South Florida, the *last* thing they usually think about is the inner city. Miami. Fort Lauderdale. Palm Beach. Boca Raton. These are the places that usually come to mind. We think of cruise ship destinations where the only thing you work on is your tan. Fantasy excursions to Key Largo. Surf, sand and fun. That's what you think if you don't live here.

Poverty Is Real

There is great poverty in South Florida. If you live here you know the area that stretches over 100 miles along the coast. On the west border, Interstate 95 marks off miles of despair. On the east side lie the railroad tracks—an unwritten barrier. This is literally the "wrong side of the tracks." If you live here you know every community along the way from Palm Beach County to Miami. You know the desolation of Overtown, where the riots burned out building after building. You know the poverty and hopelessness that dwell within. This is not a scene you will miss if you just "blink." This is a scene that you can't miss even if you want to: the crack being sold on the corners, the fear of crime that fills the air, the boarded-up buildings and abandoned dreams.

The town of Delray Beach has such a neighborhood. On the outside Delray Beach has the perquisite beaches and trendy shops, but on the inside between I-95 and the tracks, there is a different, desperate place—a neighborhood without hope.

I (Phil) have driven through this area hundreds of times. My emotions would say: "What can I do to reach them?" "I have to do something." "Can anyone really help these people?"

Then a thought struck me hard: "Jesus would do *something*."

Then Lightening Strikes

I have become all things to all men so that by all possible
means I may save some (1 Corinthians 9:22b).

It was one of those ideas you know comes from the Holy
Spirit—like a hot tropical storm: the air suddenly gets full and
heavy and it's only a matter of time till the lightening strikes. We
had been searching for a way to get into the inner city community
and affect young men's lives in a way that would have lasting
impact. We wanted them to taste how good family and relationships and Sunday morning with the church really are. We wanted
to change their lives and restore their lost hopes. As far as
community projects go, what was happening in Delray Beach
was at best nominal. Although there were some genuinely
committed individuals, you could tell they felt like they were
fighting a losing battle.

We decided to start a basketball team. We felt like the more
time we could spend with young men in their element, the more
impact we would have, but on our terms. We wanted an organization that would be excellent in every aspect. We used great
facilities. For the coaching staff we chose brothers who had
collegiate experience and who were solid spiritual men. We held
tryouts and stressed commitment to the team. We had serious
uniforms and serious practices. A few teen disciples who ex-
celled at basketball were added to the team, as were young men
with diverse racial backgrounds so that unconditional love could
be taught. We named our team "The Miami Lightening."

Then we sent the word about what we were doing out to
Washington, D.C., and soon similar teams started in Orlando,
Jacksonville, Tallahassee and Washington, D.C. We imple-
mented a plan to cover the expense of playing in these other
cities: The teams would travel together; the local church would
provide Christian families for all the young men to stay with; and
together the whole team would attend services on Sunday
mornings. The church would take care of the enthusiasm at the
afternoon games. Each young man who participated in the
league saw and experienced godly relationships every weekend.

The brochure for our program says, "Children need models more than they need critics." In the two seasons we have spent together, I only feel more strongly that this is the truth. Whether it was traveling together to Washington, D.C., or sitting in the locker room with the governor of Florida after the game, it was so much more than basketball. Staying in the homes of disciples and eating with them, we saw again and again the principle of discipleship: You must be together if people are going to see the depth of your love and commitment to God. During the actual games, the hearts of the guys, already softened by Sunday service, were encouraged by the enthusiastic crowd in a way they've probably only dreamed of.

God has made this the single, most-renowned program in Delray Beach. God has given us a chance to have an eternal impact on a few young souls because we have become involved. The impact extends even beyond the baptisms to all the young men who will see the kingdom. What thrills me the most is, like the desolate area along the tracks and I-95, there is now no way to miss the kingdom.

So often we can numb ourselves to the plight of others, but this becomes impossible when we really seek to be like Jesus. Of course we sometimes felt out-of-touch or incapable, but we strove to understand with our hearts. When we strive to be like Jesus, we see ourselves in a stranger's eyes. When we strive to be like Jesus we hear ourselves crying out in their voices. We cross over the line from *interested in* to *committed to*. The youth of the inner city will only be victorious when they have people who will be Jesus to them.

We Can Make
a Difference

21

Whatever It Takes

JIM & DONNA BLOUGH
Washington, D.C., U.S.A.

God has always had a tremendous heart for the poor. He upholds the cause of the alien, the fatherless and the widow, bringing to bear all of his miraculous power and awesome strength to see that they are treated fairly and without prejudice (Deuteronomy 10:14-19). He rejoices in the triumph of the weak—he stoops down to make the small great (2 Samuel 22:36). What an incredible principle, that the Creator of the universe is concerned about the weak and lowly among us!

Weakness Among Us

We have had a firsthand opportunity to witness God's concern for the weak and lowly in our own family. In 1987, shortly after we moved to Bombay, India, to start the church there, our youngest son Joel was diagnosed with epilepsy, which had begun to manifest itself in frequent seizures and unpredictable, often violent behavior. Joel, who had always been a sweet, adorable child, became increasingly difficult to control, often breaking things, biting and hitting his brother without cause, and demanding more and more of our attention. Trying to lead the church, disciple other churches, complete a university degree and care for a special child was an incredible challenge; but God wanted to teach us something through this. He wanted to demonstrate his love and concern for the poor and needy, and show us how he could use weakness just as powerfully as strength.

Disciples to the Rescue

First, God had already blessed us with two doctors in the Bombay church in Greg and Shelley Metten, who were a tremendous help in identifying and diagnosing Joel's condition.

Next, Pat Gempel came all the way from Boston with a new sister who was a child psychologist, just to help provide support and direction in working with Joel. Susan Hibner, a special education teacher from Chicago, and Lindy Grant, an occupational therapist from Champaign, Illinois, both agreed to move to Bombay for two years to work firsthand with Joel. Finally, Jim's mother, Jan Blough, a retired schoolteacher, was also in India with us; and she, Susan and Lindy were able to set up a special school in a neighborhood apartment just for Joel!

Doctor Needed

God had provided tremendous resources through the disciples, but professional medical attention was still required for Joel. About a month after Joel's condition was diagnosed, a search for a pediatric neurologist led us to the conclusion that there was not a single specialist in all of India who was skilled in treating child epilepsy. At that time, however, we learned of Dr. Bernard D'Souza, an Indian who had risen to Chief of Pediatrics at Duke University Medical Center, who had decided he'd had enough success in the United States and that it was time to move back to India to help his people. For two years he lived less than a mile from us, consulted with us regularly and frequently at no charge, gave us free medicine and even referred us to former colleagues. Most amazing of all, six weeks after we moved to England to serve the church there, he died of a heart attack. Apparently God moved a prominent physician halfway around the world just at the right time, to help one small boy in need.

God's Patience

After moving to England in 1989, Joel was referred to an assessment hospital where he was put through an intensive evaluation program for five days each week and was allowed to return home on weekends. What began as a six-week program stretched into six months, but during this time God was preparing our hearts to allow others to care for Joel in the way that we had always done ourselves.

When it came time for Joel to be released from care, our other son, Jesse, had changed so much that we realized it was best for Joel to live in a residential school full-time.

The Miracle House

Once we decided to search for residential schools, we quickly realized that most of the children in this type of care were much lower-functioning than Joel. We visited school after school, only to be enamored with the facilities but saddened to learn that none of the children could speak or communicate. We had finally decided if nothing opened up by March 1, 1991, we would move into a different school district to get on a three-year waiting list. On February 27, we learned of a school called Sunfield Children's Home near Birmingham. We called the headmistress and asked if we could visit on Friday, March 1, but she said we would have to come the next day (February 28—our specific prayer deadline!). We loved it and enrolled Joel immediately!

One More Miracle

In 1993 Douglas and Joyce Arthur moved to Washington, D.C., and it was obvious that it was time for us to move back to the States as well. Joel had grown so much in his school in England that we were extremely reluctant to move him, but we had come to trust God's concern for Joel and his ability to work things out. We decided to leave Joel in England for the summer while we got settled, and then bring him over in the fall when school started.

Upon our arrival, we were informed that nothing could be done to place Joel until one of the staff could interview him, but it just so happened that the Deputy Director of Special Education was going to Stratford, England, for vacation (fifty miles from Birmingham) about two weeks later. He evaluated Joel, and our son was admitted to a residential school in West Chester, Pennsylvania, before he ever reached the United States!

The Lessons

> To the LORD your God belong the heavens, even the highest heavens, the earth and everything in it.... For the LORD your God is God of gods and Lord of lords, the great God, mighty and awesome, who shows no partiality and accepts no bribes. He defends the cause of the fatherless and the widow, and loves the alien, giving him food and clothing (Deuteronomy 10:14-19).

Needless to say, we have learned a lot. Of course we bring Joel home frequently, and he is a very big part of our lives. And yes, it is challenging both to be separated from him, and also at times to be with him. But God has shown us his incredible love and concern for the weak and needy among us.

The medial staff at Joel's hospital marveled at our ability to cope with such a difficult situation, and we were able to explain to them that only through God and the church was it possible. Countless individuals have been influenced over the years by Joel and the crowd of disciples around him. Even in the face of this situation, God has raised us up to serve as an elder and women's ministry leader in his kingdom. It takes tremendous energy, devotion and mobilization of resources to serve the needy, but the rewards are incredible, both for those involved and also for those merely watching! Even though the recipients of our help are not always grateful, that's not the point. God has set an incredible standard of doing "whatever it takes" to help the poor, and as disciples of Jesus, the love of Christ leaves us no choice but to follow.

22

The Joy of Surrender

CAMERON GIFFORD
Phnom Penh, Cambodia

Empty! Worthless! Hopeless! Lonely! These feelings swirled within me on that miserable, cold and gray November morning. I was a high school senior and had just crawled out of bed around 11:00 A.M. that Saturday with a headache and feeling awful from the alcohol and marijuana I had consumed the night before. I was trying to remember the events of the previous night's party as well as sort out what I needed to do that day. Soccer season was over so I had no game or practice. I had no job. My parents were out running errands. I had no girlfriend. I had just lost my one romantic interest because I had been too afraid to pursue the relationship. My friends were out, and to be honest, I really didn't really trust them much anyway.

I looked out the window. It was so flat, so gray, so ugly, with only a few leaves moving in the cold wind. My life felt gray, too, gray and empty and meaningless. Partying and popularity were empty—my pounding head was telling me that. What was there really to look forward to? Go to college, get a job, raise a family, retire and maybe relax for a few years, and then die. Great, my life will be like every other ant on this giant anthill called Earth: empty and meaningless. I desperately wanted my life to have importance, to leave an impact—something good and noble— behind. But I was afraid. I had never done anything new or innovative. I was so cautious and fearful that many opportunities just passed me by. How could my life change into something more? How could I change to avoid the empty, antlike life?

High Hopes

Fortunately God chose me to be a disciple of Jesus and my life changed meaning and direction completely (Ephesians 1:3-14). It was incredible that my little life could now have eternal impact, that I could alter human history by helping one soul escape the sentence of hell and instead go to heaven forever (1 Thessalonians 2:19-20). Looking back I see how God unlocked my talents and abilities when I devoted them to him and not to serving my selfish desires (John 12:23-26). I discovered that serving God, the church and the lost was what made me fulfilled and happy (Acts 20:17-35). I might be tempted by fear, insecurity, pride and selfishness, but these sins would no longer control my decisions, my future and my joy. Now my decisions were made with spiritual principles, deep convictions based on God's word, and my life began to really have impact and meaning.

I approached my college studies and career with a radically different heart. I wanted to go to medical school but no longer for money, security, status and love for science. I wanted to go to be like Jesus: to help people both physically and spiritually. My grade point average at the time was low for a pre-med student and a counselor even told me I would never be accepted into medical school, but I believed that with God's Spirit, I could do the work.

> From everyone who has been given much, much will be demanded; and from the one who has been entrusted with much, much more will be asked (Luke 12:48b).

God gives us each various talents. I knew he had entrusted me with much and that he would be more pleased if I tried and failed than if I never tried (Luke 12:41-48). I also could not stand the thought of living with my cowardice the rest of my life. I reasoned that if I did not get accepted to medical school then God had a far better plan for me and my career in his kingdom (Matthew 7:7-11). I prayed, worked very hard and gave my first fruits to God. He blessed me with straight A's for three semesters and later acceptance into medical school (Malachi 3:6-12). The key here was surrender to God (Luke 9:23-25). I would have been happy to do whatever he wanted me to do.

Throughout the years of medical school, internship and private practice, I have persevered in following God. Twice I almost fell away because I wavered in my commitment to Jesus.

I began to focus on my wants and the way I thought things should happen, and I had to surrender. But God blessed my repentance richly. First by giving me an awesome wife, Chiara, and then in using us to help build a new church that saved many souls. Even at this point, once more I tried to take the reins back and steer my life where I wanted to go. Once more God won, and I again surrendered. God has since worked to knit our family into a loving, unified and fruitful household. God also gave us a growing suburban ministry which has converted future leaders. God always blesses us. Throughout the years God has given us new challenges, and then after our surrender, he has given us the specific talents to get the job done. We both now have talents that never existed before we came into the kingdom.

As my wife and I, along with our three children, journey to Phnom Penh, Cambodia, to help start the new Sihanouk Hospital center of HOPE, I again have to surrender fear, doubt, insecurity and materialism to God. Some in our families persecute us for going to such a ridiculous place. Some of my medical colleagues have laughed at me or ridiculed me behind my back. My associates challenged my leaving the practice because it hurt their financial interests. Fortunately, trust in God is so much easier this time. This is where God wants me—surrendered and on the edge so he can bless me with new talents for his glory and the glory of his kingdom. My life has truly been saved forever from that empty way of life handed down to me.

23

When I Go to Work,
I'm Gonna Let It Shine

DAVE MALUTINOK
Philadelphia, U.S.A.

Jesus expects us as disciples to make a difference in our spheres of influence. He means for us to shine and draw others to him and to his heart for the poor.

> "You are the light of the world. A city on a hill cannot be hidden. Neither do people light a lamp and put it under a bowl. Instead they put it on its stand, and it gives light to everyone in the house. In the same way, let your light shine before men, that they may see your good deeds and praise your Father in heaven" (Matthew 5:14-16).

Many disciples underestimate the influence they have, or could have, in receiving substantial donations to be given to the charity of their choice. Loyal, hardworking employees are appreciated by their management and therefore are respected when they call their companies to support fund-raisers and matching-donation programs. Many corporations are looking for a conduit to help the community through budgeted benevolence. If there is an opportunity to give to an organization about which little is known, versus an organization which one of their star employees supports, which do you think a corporation will choose? The same goes for our neighbors, friends and family. Put your lamp on the stand, and use your influence for God's glory.

Joseph is a great example of using his influence in his circle of acquaintances. His integrity, righteousness and hard work won the favor of his employees—Potiphar, the head jailer and Pharaoh himself. (You can read the story in Genesis 39-41.) Because of Joseph's favorable status, his "boss" allowed him to do what was necessary to meet the physical needs of many people who would have otherwise died in the seven-year famine.

Patience and Perseverance

Although you may be trying to be a model employee, you may find yourself feeling that your influence is not appreciated. You may even find yourself frustrated that you are suffering certain types of persecution. Again, look at Joseph's life. It had been God's plan to use Joseph powerfully to save the Israelite nation, but he first had to go through some character adjustments. God gave him a number of challenging life situations to prepare him for his powerful work of service. Be patient, pray and persevere. And by all means, do not stop seeking excellence as an employee, for that is God's will for you whether you feel appreciated or not.

We tend to think that when we are part of something that will help the poor, others will roll out the red carpet, blow the trumpets and welcome the help with open arms. Unfortunately, helping the poor is not so easy. Our society has a mistrust of those who are truly wanting to help. So many times bright assurances turn into empty promises. Those awaiting the promises are hurt and let down, so they no longer trust anyone. They want to see action before opening up their hearts. Helping the poor takes patient endurance—the type of endurance only God builds in our character. God had to build that patient character in Joseph through his unjust suffering. In Genesis 39 Joseph was thrown into prison for being righteous. In Genesis 40 Joseph helped a noble's official, only to be forgotten and treated with ingratitude. In both of these events, Joseph could have held a pity party for himself; instead, he resolved to continue doing his best, and eventually (after thirteen years) rose to a powerful position. In God's timing, after he learned the lessons of patience and faith, he became the ruler over all of Egypt. He then had the power and authority to help the poor, beginning with his own people, through a devastating famine.

I remember having the ambitious desire to help orphans through adoption. *Surely all government officials will have the same desire,* I thought. *HOPE for Children will be welcomed with open arms.* But instead, I was met with skepticism, distrust and lethargy. Thankfully, through God's direction and our perseverance, we were able to find those who really had a heart to help orphans in their countries. I believe that God wanted to see how strong our desire was. Once he trusted our perseverance, he opened the doors, and more than seventy orphans were adopted in less than three years.

God's Blessing

It is inspiring to see how Joseph used the wisdom he had gained through his difficult circumstances. The end result was that God gave him the insight to plan a strategy that saved a nation. Joseph ended up using all of his talents and strengths to glorify God powerfully.

In much the same way God has blessed the growth and effectiveness of HOPE *worldwide.* In fact, many people in non-profit circles are amazed at the growth from sponsoring three projects in 1991 to sponsoring multiple projects in more than a hundred cities in 1996. There are two reasons for this: (1) God, pure and simple! He is the one with the most compassionate heart for the poor...just look at the life of Jesus. (2) The perseverance of the people of God. It is amazing to see the quality of people God has chosen to help the poor at HOPE. With leaders like Bob and Pat Gempel, the geographic HOPE vice presidents and all the project leaders throughout the world, it's no wonder that our growth has been so phenomenal. Of equal importance are the 60,000-plus volunteers of HOPE—no volunteers of any organization are more dedicated, joyful or talented.

How blessed it is when disciples have the opportunity, whether as full-time employees or part-time volunteers, to pour out their lives and energies to meet the needs of the poor and to encourage those in their spheres of influence to do the same. In so doing, they truly give light to all who are in the world.

24

Athletic Gifts for a Lasting Crown

MIKE SHERIDAN
Philadelphia, U.S.A.

While watching an NFL playoff game during the Christmas holidays, a friend visiting from Australia commented how enormous the professional sports business is in North America. This is no revelation for those of us who live in the U.S.A. (*Unlimited Sports Anytime*). Team owners spend millions on players, sponsors spend millions on television advertising and we spend millions on our wide screen TVs and sports jackets and stadium seats to watch our "heroes" compete in the games. While such games elicit greater zeal and allegiance in the hearts of their followers than the stale, tradition-bound "Christianity" of our day, they often produce little of lasting value for either those who compete or those who watch.

New Testament Athletics

The pages of the New Testament, particularly the writings of Paul, are full of references to sports and physical training. On the one hand, Paul knew both the limited good of physical exercise (1 Timothy 4:8) and the temporary fulfillment of athletic victory (1 Corinthians 9:25). However, Paul found in athletic competition a number of powerful metaphors for those living for Christ. As Paul made use of athletics to communicate spiritual lessons, we are seeing today that many disciples are learning to use their athletic abilities to advance God's purposes in our world. If one's aim in competing is to gain honor for self, then the result is worthless even if the gold is won. However, if one can use sports or any other talent to show God's love and compassion to the lost world, then the result will be eternal.

> Each one should use whatever gift he has received to serve others, faithfully administering God's grace in it's various forms (1 Peter 4:10).

Peter reveals that the very reason we receive gifts from God is to serve other people. Those gifted with athletic skills and abilities can use them to help others to find salvation and to meet various physical and emotional needs of the poor and needy. It is exciting to see the number of highly accomplished athletes from all around the globe making their decision to put Jesus first and begin to use their God-given talent to advance the kingdom. Consider just a few of the things that have been done, particularly to show God's love to the poor:

- Just three miles from the HOPE *worldwide* main office in Philadelphia, troubled teens live hopeless lives—victims of abuse, neglect and abandonment. Once a week the HOPE basketball team, also known as "HOOP *worldwide*," plays games and builds relationships with the teens and counselors in that area.

- Since 1993 the HOPE Golf Classic in Miami has been bringing together professional golfers, enthusiastic disciples and major international corporations to raise thousands of dollars in support of HOPE projects in Central and South America. Many poor in Mexico and Brazil have seen dreams realized because of this annual event.

- Disciples in Miami also established the HOPE basketball program for inner-city youth (discussed in Chapter 20). Through the coaching, mentoring, tutoring and friendship provided by volunteers, teenagers are being provided with godly role models—something so desperately needed today. The Miami Lightening basketball program has become a bright light in a city famous for its deeds of darkness.

- In 1996 HOPE developed a world-class athletic competition to raise money for HOPE for Kids, their nationwide immunization and child healthcare outreach. On April 19 six solo riders and eight teams took their place at the starting line in Boston for the first annual HOPE for Kids FundRACE. This 500-mile bicycle race was sanctioned by the Ultramarathon Cycling Association as the east coast qualifier for the prestigious Race Across AMerica (RAAM). *Outside* magazine called the RAAM the most challenging ultrasport in the world, as its competitors race 3000 miles across the United States in just eight days. In its first year the FundRACE featured RAAM champions Rob Kish ('94, '95), Danny Chew ('96), Australian Gerry Tatrai ('93) and George Thomas ('93 Team RAAM). These racers covered the course in under thirty hours as they raced nonstop from Boston to Washington D.C. After the race the professional competitors said they were amazed at the zealous, warm and helpful spirit of all the race volunteers. Some said it was the best race they'd ever competed in. Even more impressive than the professionals' performances was the heart of the amateur teams. Each of the eight teams were composed of disciples who had never raced in an ultramarathon race in their lives. Yet their love for the "games" combined with their desire to help the poor drove them through the momentous emotional and physical challenges of the race.

Don't Leave the Talent—Use It!

Just like musical and artistic talent, athletic ability is a tremendous gift from God. Disciples have used this gift to develop character, build relationships in the kingdom and to reach out to others who need the message of Jesus. But how much have you used your athletic gift to help the poor and needy? Look around and see the hurting people in your neighborhoods, towns and cities. Remember God's word teaches that each of us should use our gifts to serve others, administering his grace in *all* its various forms.

In Luke 5:1-11 we see that Peter sacrificially left his boat on the beach to follow Jesus. However, we see in the same passage that Jesus was able to use that discarded boat (asset) to preach the

Word from. Have you left behind the athletic talents or any other asset that God has given you? Jesus can and wants to use that talent to accomplish his will. Perhaps you are only using these gifts for the "spiritual" purpose of seeking the lost, forgetting Jesus' own words that when we serve the needs of the poor, we are actually serving him (Matthew 25:34-46).

Get back in the games, disciples. Start up the strict training. Use that athletic talent and determination not for self-glory but to bring a cure to the hurting people around you. Work for the crown that will last forever.

25

Is It Legal?

RANDY & JAN JORDAN
Washington, D.C., U.S.A.

The apostle Paul had nearly exhausted all the possibilities for relief as his body lay stretched across the rack, about to be flogged. Only hours earlier, Paul had been undergoing Jewish rites of purification at the temple in Jerusalem as an extraordinary step to demonstrate his obedience to the law. But some Jews from the province of Asia had recognized him in the temple. They spread lies about him which led ultimately to his arrest by Roman soldiers.

In his defense, Paul spoke persuasively about his heritage as a Jew and his miraculous experience on the road to Damascus, which led to his baptism by Ananias. He explained passionately about his role in the death of Stephen and his extraordinary calling by God to preach the Gospel to the Gentiles.

His arguments, however, fell on deaf ears, and Paul found himself about to undergo an interrogation by torture. As Paul's body strained against the chains which held him captive, his mind raced, searching for any possible means of escape. The centurion made final preparations for the brutal beating, and Paul spoke one final time, hoping for a last-minute reprieve from his punishment. He said, *"Is it legal* for you to flog a Roman citizen who hasn't even been found guilty?"* (Acts 22:25, emphasis added). Paul's plaintive cry quickly made its way from the ears of the centurion to the attention of the Roman commander. Within minutes the interrogators retreated, and Paul's inquisition was abruptly ended.

When Paul's immense powers of persuasion failed to convince his Roman captors, God used Paul's legal status as a Roman citizen to bring about his rescue. The teachers of the law, who sought Paul's death for alleged violations of the Jewish law, were beaten at their own game as Paul posed the simple question to the Roman guards, "Is it legal?"

Helpful Laws

> Everyone must submit himself to the governing authorities, for there is no authority except that which God has established. The authorities that exist have been established by God (Romans 13:1).

While our initial reaction may be to think unkindly towards governmental restrictions and requirements, the laws of the land can provide Christians with advantages as we strive to meet the needs of the poor. Of course, in matters of faith we must join the ranks of Paul and the early apostles. When confronted with strict orders from the Sanhedrin to stop teaching about Jesus, they responded in Acts 5:29, "We must obey God rather than men!" In most instances, however, the guidance provided by Paul in Romans 13:1 is appropriate.

In providing legal assistance to HOPE *worldwide* we have become aware of numerous instances when God has used the laws of the governing authorities to assist disciples in meeting the needs of the poor. For example, we rejoice that the adoption agency, HOPE for Children, has been able to place more than a hundred homeless and abandoned children into Christian homes during the past five years. These adoptions were made possible through licenses issued by the governing authorities in the state of Georgia and the countries of Honduras, India and the People's Republic of China. Through HOPE for Children the desires of God for homeless children in Psalms 68:6 can be fulfilled: "God sets the lonely in families."

We observed another example on a recent trip to Phnom Penh, Cambodia. Due to the ravages of war and civil unrest, Cambodia is one of the most medically underserved nations in the world. Yet, HOPE is now able to deliver much-needed medical services to the people of Cambodia through a new hospital authorized and supported by the King of Cambodia. The Sihanouk Hospital center of HOPE provides outpatient and inpatient health care services to thousands of Cambodians and functions as a training facility for scores of Cambodian national medical personnel. Without the support of the Cambodian authorities, the construction of this state-of-the-art medical facility would not have been possible.

Similarly, the tax-exemption laws and charitable solicitation statutes in the United States permit HOPE *worldwide*, as an approved charitable organization, to seek additional funding for its projects from private and public sponsors. HOPE's ability to meet the healthcare education needs of inner city parents in the United States through the nationally recognized HOPE for Kids program is due in part to HOPE's ability to raise funds under the authority of these laws. In April 1996 we joined thousands of HOPE for Kids volunteers in distributing vital information about the importance of childhood immunizations to parents of more than one million inner city children.

God's Law on Our Hearts

God recognized the role of laws in maintaining the righteousness of the Hebrew people when he offered Moses the first installment of the book of the law on Mount Sinai. With thunder, lightning and smoke, God etched the Ten Commandments into two tablets of stone and instructed Moses, "These are the laws you are to set before them" (Exodus 21:1). God knew that his people needed a clear definition of right and wrong in order to avoid the damaging sin-traps of Satan. The apostle Paul acknowledged this need in Romans 7:7 when he declared, "Indeed I would not have known what sin was except through the law. For I would not have known what coveting really was if the law had not said, 'Do not covet.'"

While the establishment of the Law clarified the existence of sin for the Hebrews, it did little to resolve the consequences of their sin. Thus, God's people were burdened with the limitations of the law until God provided a more complete solution to the problem of sin. In Galatians 3:24-25, Paul describes the long-awaited perfect solution, "So the law was put in charge to lead us to Christ that we might be justified by faith. Now that faith has come, we are no longer under the supervision of the law."

As the ultimate authority behind all earthly laws, God has provided a legal means through HOPE *worldwide* for twentieth-century Christians to be able to meet the needs of the poor and disadvantaged. When HOPE is asked the question, "Is it legal?", we answer with a resounding, "Yes!"

On a personal level, however, we find that the question of legality is not the most probing one, for God does not measure our service to the poor under the standard of the law. Instead, God evaluates our service under a standard of faith and righteousness, knowing that only righteous and faith-filled hearts will care enough to meet the challenges of a needy world. Have you been faithful to God's plan for you in this area of service?

26
Kids Who Care

EDDIE & ROXANNE ARMES
Boston, U.S.A.

What is the HOPE Youth Corps? What is its purpose? To see another country? To help the poor? To build relationships with other teens and campus students in the kingdom? To learn to be focused on others and be grateful? Answer: All of the above! We have been so grateful to be a part of this exciting program designed for teenagers and campus students to experience a totally different side of life: to experience new countries, cultures, food, people and, most of all, to see, smell, sense and feel firsthand the needs of the poor and needy; to come face to face with people in third-world countries and to learn to meet their needs.

The 1996 HOPE Youth Corps theme was "Planet Youth Corps—HOPE for the Planet!" Planning six projects in six different third-world countries was quite a task, but HOPE for the Planet became a reality. Let us tell you a little bit about how the Youth Corps helped other people everywhere.

Mexico City, Mexico

Forty-five teenage volunteers from all over the world worked with an impoverished mountain community to build a one-room school house for their children. The bricks had to be carried up the mountain one by one by means of a human chain—incredible team work! The group assisted in washing dirty hands and faces and helped feed over a hundred street children a day. The teens put on a daily carnival, played games and made crafts. Each team member brought a huge bag of clothes, shoes and toys which were distributed to the children. What an incredible sight to see nearly two hundred dirty children with ragged clothing lined up to receive a new outfit and a pair of shoes. To see smiles appear on those little faces was worth the world to us all! At the CASA clinic the group played games, face-painted and brought joy to the hearts of all the children waiting to see the doctors.

One particularly touching sight involved a six-year-old girl who was joining in the fun with the other children. She was playing a game and having a great time. Suddenly one of the other children grabbed her arm and pointed to a twelve-month-old baby crying on the curb. I had been trying to comfort the baby to no avail. The little girl quickly walked over to her baby brother, pulled out a dirty bottle of water, put his head on her lap and comforted him. I thought it was so sweet of her. Then I looked at her little face. It was caked with dirt and tears were streaming down her cheeks. It was then that I began to grasp the incredibly hard life these children live. She just wanted to join in the game and have fun, yet she was responsible to care for her baby brother all day while her mom was at work.

Abidjan, Ivory Coast

The youths worked in two slum areas, providing clothes, shoes and toys to the children in Abidjan. They also worked at a hospital bathing AIDS patients. One man whom the volunteers helped to bathe was so touched by the kindness that he could not stop crying. This man had been bedridden in a hospital and had bed sores all over his body. It was extremely painful to be bathed. The teens felt bad and thought he was crying because of the pain. He later explained that he was so moved that someone would care enough to touch him. He had not been bathed for four months. Not even his own daughter was willing to come and help him.

Hong Kong

In Hong Kong the Youth Corp helped the elderly clean their homes. Strong young men and women cleaned places that had been collecting dust and dirt for years. These older people were overjoyed to have energetic youths helping them. Such simple efforts warmed many hearts. The group also worked very hard to decorate a therapy room at a local hospital. What a transformation from a cold, white room to a bright, cheerful display! Now this room not only gives therapy but lifts the spirits of all who enter it.

Bangalore, India

We had all seen many pictures and video footage of India, but nothing compared to being there, smelling it and seeing it with our own eyes. The Youth Corp team went out each day determined to give to the Indian people. Sometimes they gave clothing and other times nutritional supplements to help the malnourished children. We will never forget walking into a shack and being handed a nine-month-old baby who was so severely malnourished he weighed only ten pounds. His eyes were glassy and his mouth was wide open as he gasped for breath. As he looked into my eyes, my heart broke for him and all of the other children living in poverty in India.

Kingston, Jamaica

The group brought joy to an orphanage full of beautiful little Jamaican children. They cleaned and painted the HOPE Vouch Clinic. At the Glenhope Place of Safety (an orphanage) they completely furnished the library with children's books and toys. At the Mona Rehabilitation Center they played and spent time with all of the disabled children. One of the disabled girls, who was a teenager herself, was so sad when the group arrived, but by the end of the visit she was smiling.

Bucharest, Romania

Casa de Copii Nr. 4, one of many orphanages in Bucharest, received a face-lift from the Youth Corps. The walls surrounding the building's play area were very drab. When the youths finished painting, the area was bright and beautiful! Inside they painted and wallpapered several areas including an indoor play room. More importantly, the teens provided much-needed love to each child in the orphanage. The climax of the project was a huge carnival at the orphanage including "Christmas in July"! The orphans had a great time and each received a brightly wrapped gift that had been provided by members of the Boston Church of Christ who have "adopted" a special child. The teens also spent a day preparing meals which they bagged and took throughout the city to feed the street children. Each teen had brought a bag of clothes which were sorted and given to these children on the streets. One little girl, with head shaved, smiled and danced when her tattered T-shirt was replaced by a beautiful dress. Everyone, children and adults, experienced the joy of abundant love.

Examples for the Believers

Don't let anyone look down on you because you are young, but set an example for the believers in speech, in life, in love, in faith and in purity (1 Timothy 4:12).

The young men and women who served in the HOPE Youth Corps learned so much about the countries, the culture and the people they visited. Each life they touched left a lasting impact on their own heart for the poor. The relationships they built with these people and among themselves will last a lifetime.

Teenagers, in particular, are surrounded by temptations to be ungrateful, self-centered and self-absorbed. The Youth Corps takes them out of their comfortable environment and puts them in a third-world country, surrounded by needs that are so obvious! It softened their hearts to the point of being able to see how grateful we all need to be for shelter, food, clothing, family, love, care and even the smallest blessings of life. They grew in their own character and serve as godly examples "in speech, in life, in love, in faith and in purity" to peers and adults alike.

27

Start When They Are Young

GREG & SHELLEY METTEN
Los Angeles, U.S.A.

STAN & BETTY MOREHEAD
Boston, U.S.A.

Jennifer and Claire were making their way to a small apartment in a village in the Middle East where a group was preparing to discuss the Bible. As they reached a government checkpoint, they were stopped, questioned and told that they could not go any further because of rioting that was taking place. As they boarded the bus to return to their apartment, they could hear the sounds of gunfire and sirens blaring in the distance. Fear gripped them both when they realized that some of their closest friends were living right in the middle of the worst fighting. However, they reassured each other by recalling other harrowing adventures they had experienced together. As this book goes to press these two college students and special friends are part of a tiny minority following Christ in the land where he once lived and where he cared for the souls and bodies of those in need.

Childhood Friends

Claire and Jennifer's friendship began in 1985 when Jennifer, her parents (Greg and Shelley), and her brother, Matthew, left San Diego (and their careers) to train for a mission team being sent out by a church of disciples in Boston. Stan and Betty Morehead, who were a part of this church, asked the Metten family to stay with them and their children, Claire and Graham, for several days while they looked for housing. A bond developed that would last a lifetime. Although the Mettens stayed in Boston for only a year before going to Bombay, India, their families' relationship grew because both were committed to the same goal: helping the world to be evangelized in their generation.

Friendships born out of a shared goal are the ones that stand the test of time. The Mettens left for India in September 1986, and although the two families were separated by ten thousand miles, the children continued to write to one another. Then, in the summer of 1988, Graham (16) and Claire (13) stayed with Jennifer (13) and Matt (12) in Bombay. This was a sacrifice for both the Moreheads and the Mettens, but God blessed it incredibly.

The children's friendships deepened as they traveled the streets of Bombay observing the poor, exploring the markets and making new friends with the Indian people. Their experience would help to shape their own convictions one day about their personal need to imitate the life of Jesus and to help others to do the same.

Lasting Impression

It didn't matter whether they lived in Boston or Bombay; to our kids, the kingdom of God has always been one new adventure after another, and they have always loved being a part of it. They love it because we love it. You can't fool your kids. They observe you at church, and especially at home, and they know where your heart truly is. They hear the words, whether faithful or critical, and they watch how you spend your time: in front of the television or at the dinner table sharing your food and faith with friends.

> Love the LORD your God with all your heart and with all your soul and with all your strength. These commandments that I give you today are to be upon your hearts. Impress them on your children. Talk about them when you sit at home and when you walk along the road, when you lie down and when you get up. Tie them as symbols on your hands and bind them on your foreheads. Write them on the doorframes of your houses and on your gates (Deuteronomy 6:5-9).

Our example is incredibly important. From a very young age our children observe us and want to imitate us. If we are of a critical nature or pessimistic, they will become that way. If we are hypocritical, they will see through us sooner or later and lose heart. But, if we have a zeal for God and are really trying to apply his principles in parenting and in all aspects of our lives, they will be encouraged and secure.

We must constantly examine ourselves by observing our kids and what they really get excited about. Do they love spending time with kids who love God and his church, or are they attracted to those who are disrespectful toward authority and make fun of people? "Do not be misled: 'Bad company corrupts good character'" (1 Corinthians 15:33). It is our job as parents to make sure that life in the kingdom of God is much more fun and appealing than life in the world.

Youth Corps

Every summer while the Mettens were overseas, Jennifer and Matthew would travel back to the U.S. to visit their grand-parents and friends. Again, this required considerable financial sacrifice and extensive planning, but it was worth the cost. They were able to help other teenagers who were undergoing spiritual challenges as well as receive encouragement themselves. These teenage friendships became so important that when the Mettens moved back to the States in 1991, the first thing they did was to plan a reunion over Easter break with some of their children's closest friends. What began as a few days with the Moreheads and a few others, quickly mushroomed into twenty-five kids from all over the country converging on the Mettens' home for three great days of fun and fellowship. In reality this was the mustard seed beginning of the HOPE Youth Corps (see the previous chapter), where today kids from all over the kingdom share fellowship, faith and a commitment to helping others.

Our kids have been an incredible source of inspiration and joy to us as parents through the years. We have seen them grow and mature and, yes, they have had their challenging times. But there was never any doubt that they would one day become committed Christians, which they have. They love God with all their hearts and have an "overwhelming positive outlook on their future," as Graham recently stated. They know that they will one day marry other committed Christians and raise children that love God as much as they do.

> "For I have chosen him, so that he will direct his children and his household after him to keep the way of the LORD by doing what is right and just, so that the LORD will bring about for Abraham what he has promised him" (Genesis 18:19).

With God's help we must direct our children to do "what is right and just," so that they can inherit the incredible promise of being part of the kingdom of God!

28

Purity of Purpose

ERICA KIM
Tokyo, Japan

In the fall of 1995, my brother Hiroshi was working late at his job in New York City. Before leaving for home, he phoned to tell his wife, Mayo, "I'm happy and I love you." Several hours later, the police called to report that he had been in an accident. Hiroshi was already dead when they found him; he most likely had fallen asleep at the wheel.

I cannot tell you the anguish and pain that all of us felt upon hearing the news. He was only thirty years old. At the funeral, it was so hard to explain to my three-year-old nephew what had happened to his daddy. Hiroaki kept hovering over the coffin and shaking my brother saying, "Daddy, wake up. Daddy, wake up." My sister-in-law was in shock. My father did not say a word to me from the time my brother died until after the funeral, at which point he burst into tears. At such times there are no words sufficient to comfort.

During this period, no one in my family was in any condition to do anything except feel deep sorrow for the loss of Hiroshi. I admire my husband, Frank, for taking charge when none of us could. He was already thinking about Mayo and Hiroaki's future. The night before the funeral we talked for a long time about what we could do for them. His love and concern for my family prompted him to decide that it would be best for them to move in with us. Frank was practicing religion that James would say is "pure and faultless" (James 1:27). As a result of that decision, three months later Mayo was baptized into Christ! God is so faithful. Although I had lost a brother, I gained a sister.

The last few months have been incredibly miraculous months for our family. Mayo has become a fruitful leader and is now dating a brother who is on staff. In addition to that, she was able to share with the Tokyo church how her tragedy had helped her to understand the cross in a profound way. Her life is having an impact that can be felt throughout the entire church.

Responding to the Need

Life is full of tragedy and times of difficulty. Our response to these times in the lives of others measures the sacrificial attitudes of our heart. Jesus was very aggressive in helping those in need. As soon as he saw the widow of Nain mourning the death of her only son, his heart went out to her. (See Luke 7:12-16.) What spurs our heart to go out to others? Do the tears of others stir compassion in us? Does the pain of another person fill us with a longing to comfort them in their distress?

Often, we allow our busy schedules and demanding responsibilities to impede us from responding to the desperate needs of others. I admire people like Scott and Lynne Green and Doug and Joyce Arthur. They have some of the most strenuous schedules and life-styles in the kingdom of God. But their responsibilities have not hindered each family from reaching out to adopt an orphan.

I was especially touched by something Lynne shared about her new Chinese daughter, Ariel. Even though she had never met Ariel's birth mother, she felt a special bond to her. This young woman was only fourteen when she gave birth! With tears in her eyes, Lynne shared about how much she wanted to meet Ariel's true mother and share the gospel with her. She wanted Ariel to someday be able to have the joy of knowing that her physical mother was saved as well as her adoptive mother. Truly, I felt a deep selfless love in Lynne's tears.

Our sympathy can dry the tears of another when we reach out and touch their lives. Are we able to feel *with* others like Jesus did? Like many other committed disciples have? We need to ask ourselves, "Do I *feel* compassion for others?" "Can I relate?" That loving kindness can transform someone's life.

Our Motivation to Give

If I give all I possess to the poor and surrender my body to the flames, but have not love, I gain nothing (1 Corinthians 13:3).

Many of us do try to help the poor. We put aside money and even sacrifice on a weekly basis for the needy. Has it, however, become a habit? Is it just an organizational function? Is the heart still behind those acts of righteousness?

This scripture basically tells us that some people are capable of giving everything—even their lives—for others but still are without love. There is no gain in giving if our hearts are not behind the contribution. What a waste of time and energy when we impart gifts to others in obligation rather than in true concern.

Often, it is those who have personally experienced pain and suffering that possess the deepest form of compassion. Even if they do not have much, they give all that they can to help others. Many also give out of gratitude for what was done for them or for someone they loved.

After the death of my brother, Frank and I took a missionary journey/scouting trip to refresh our spirits. On our trip to Hokkaido, the northern island of Japan, Frank was reading a newspaper in which there was a small article asking for aid to North Korean flood victims. For us, it was an exciting opportunity because we have wanted to help North Korea in some way through HOPE *worldwide*. Through this project to send rice to North Korea, Frank was able to build a bond with Bernie Krisher, former bureau chief of *Newsweek* in Tokyo. Bernie is a man dedicated to benevolence. Out of appreciation for the support given his family in escaping the Nazi occupation of Europe, Bernie decided to become involved in charity work himself.

Bernie actually was the person who began the hospital project in Cambodia written about in Chapters 3, 6 and 22. The Sihanouk Hospital center of HOPE will be an around-the-clock, free hospital for anyone needing treatment in Phnom Penh. It will also be a training center for a new generation of Cambodian doctors.

Jesus Is Our Example

Jesus has given us the heart and understanding necessary to meet the needs of others. His purity of purpose has enabled so many disciples through the centuries to extend a helping hand to those less fortunate than themselves. In growing closer to our Lord, our charity for others should never decrease but always increase. As we live out the purpose of seeking and saving the lost, let us remember we must always sustain a purity in our purpose. The sincerely compassionate heart will certainly bear much fruit for the Lord...in every way.

29

Unity of the Believers

STEVE JOHNSON
New York City, U.S.A.

Before Calvin died I got one more phone call. With his kind of cancer we had long stopped praying that God would make him better. We just prayed that it would please be over for him soon, thank you, Jesus. Next thing you know you're getting the phone calls.

"The doctors say that radiation won't help anymore."

"This is it. They just give him a few more days to be with us."

"I know you're busy, but could you come down and see him in the hospital?"

Life seems so long, and all of a sudden it's only a few days and a bunch of phone calls.

I went down and sat by him on one of those beds that you never want to think about ending up on yourself. I don't remember much about that talk, only that when I left I knew I'd never see him again.

A couple of days later I got another phone call from his wife, Joyce. "He's asked them to turn off the IV."

Calvin's IV was an electrolyte and nutrient cocktail meant to prolong his life. He had asked to speak to his doctor alone, without Joyce, because he wanted to know if he would ever go home again. The doctor said no and that his IV was keeping him alive. Calvin said to turn the thing off.

"Are you okay?" I lamely asked Joyce over the phone.

"I thought I was ready but I'm not. How about you?"

"Me? I'm fine, it's just..."

"Just what?"

"I made some reservations to fly down and see him again."

I hung up knowing that in the next few days I'd be getting that other phone call telling me that it was time for the funeral. But not five minutes later the phone rang.

"Steve, can you come on down here now?"

The irony that we had been on the phone just seconds before and now he was dead choked me until Joyce calmly spoke again.

"I told Calvin that you had plans to come see him."

"Yeah?"

"He told them to start the IV back up."

The Bible says that greater love has no man than to lay down his life for a friend. But what do you call *refusing* to die so you can see somebody one more time?

So our last conversation was about a friend who had decided to leave our fellowship.

"He just doesn't get it," Calvin said. "If we don't stick together, we'll never make it."

Submission Is Powerful

I believe Calvin made it, and the legacy he left me was a vow to unity, a vow to stick together, to "get it."

One of the secrets of the universe is this: *Voluntary submission is powerful*. In Ephesians 5:21 ("Submit to one another out of reverence to Christ...") Paul commands us to give in to each other. Not an easy thing for mortals, but then he motivates us with the nudge "...out of reverence to Christ." He doesn't say to submit to another brother or sister only when they are being spiritual giants and biblical geniuses. He simply says to submit.

If we could see submission like a traffic intersection with a four-way stop then maybe we could understand that God commands us to yield in order to avoid bad accidents. Everyone eventually gets a turn when everyone submits to one another. This creates unity, and unity provides the climate necessary for the Holy Spirit to do his work.

Nothing has demonstrated this principle in the church more than our experience with Hope for Kids. Originally an immunization drive in Orlando, we found a niche for serving in the metro New York area by knocking doors and reaching out to folks who don't usually have assistance getting their children immunized.

The story would have ended with one successful weekend project in Harlem if not for the unity among churches across America. In one year's time Hope for Kids went from being an outreach in one city promoted by three-thousand volunteers to a coast to coast campaign over thirty-thousand strong. Hope for Kids then was able to make such a splash that corporations and official health organizations have been eager to partner with us in helping children in nearly every state of the United States.

Because disciples of Jesus are willing to be united and work together, Hope for Kids has become what Bud Chiles, Hope for Kids director of New York, called "the Ford Foundation with teeth." We're united. We show up. We don't quit and we're not afraid to work for others. And we want God to get the credit.

Just as our flesh is tempted in many ways to be arrogant and proud, divisive and cynical, our spirit longs to be righteous and united in eternal pursuits. I'm as likely as anyone to get a bad attitude when someone's desire to boss me around clashes with my opinion or seems to be speeding towards a head-on collision with common sense.

But how can we honestly think we have any chance at living forever with God in heaven if we can't live with each other for just a little while here on Earth? We need motivation for the times when we don't feel like participating in something "bigger than ourselves" or when someone is not leading just the way we think they should be. We need to remember Jesus and submit to each other on our "bad hair, bad prayer" days. We need to be able to think of the people who have sacrificed for us and be inspired to get moving and do something for someone else.

For me, motivation is pretty easy. I can think about Calvin—how he wouldn't die until he'd seen me one last time just to talk about unity.

Just to make sure before he left that I "got it."

30
What Must I Do?

MOHAN & HELEN NANJUNDAN
Delhi, India

It was a warm summer morning in the southern Indian city of Hyderabad, home to five million people. We had arrived in the city a few hours earlier and were excited to get a firsthand view of the work for the poor being done by the HOPE *worldwide* staff there. Hyderabad is a city with a thriving construction industry. The building boom has attracted the rural poor into this metropolis in droves, including many from India's colorful Banjara (itinerant gypsy) community,

For the poor these opportunities to work are a mixed blessing. There are jobs on the building sites, but most are only temporary. Workers are migratory and have to frequently move from site to site, families in tow. The conditions on the sites are often dangerous and the risk of accidents is ever-present, as well as obvious health hazards associated with dust and pollution. The children of the workers are malnourished, illiterate and constantly uprooted. Food is abundant, but expensive, in the city. Dreams here die fast for the poor.

Daily Grind

We visited two work sites: one is in a remote area, the other downtown. HOPE workers serve at four construction sites in the city, educating the children and helping with basic medical needs, especially malnutrition. The children were always smiling, chattering and full of life. There was something these children understood that often escapes us grown-ups—that joy is not equal to the sum total of your possessions!

Fathers and mothers both work at the construction sites. Poor women frequently do very heavy labor. A few grandmothers were present and were delighted to meet us. We looked around at their homes—dwellings made of sticks, rags and torn plastic sheeting. Inside nothing but a few cooking utensils, no toys, no sign of anything but the most basic of basics. We have seen homes like this many times in our work, yet we still choke on our tears.

The realness of the people we met that morning remains indelibly etched on our hearts and minds. We felt one with them. What struck us the most was that there was no real difference between us and them. Only by the grace of God were we so fortunate in life, while these families faced such terrible hardship. We felt very undeserving and so very blessed. It was a wake-up call to gratefulness!

A Jesus Wake-up Call

Experiences like this inevitably result in different responses. Either you can harden your heart to the needs of others, allowing selfishness to scar your very soul; or you can wake up to the call of discipleship, seek Jesus and ask yourself the question: What must I do?

> As Jesus started on his way, a man ran up to him and fell on his knees before him. "Good teacher," he asked, "what must I do to inherit eternal life?"
>
> "Why do you call me good?" Jesus answered. "No one is good—except God alone. You know the commandments: 'Do not murder, do not commit adultery, do not steal, do not give false testimony, do not defraud, honor your father and mother.'"
>
> "Teacher," he declared, "all these I have kept since I was a boy."
>
> Jesus looked at him and loved him. "One thing you lack," he said. "Go, sell everything you have and give to the poor, and you will have treasure in heaven. Then come, follow me."
>
> At this the man's face fell. He went away sad, because he had great wealth (Mark 10:17-22).

When the rich young ruler asked "What must I do?", Jesus' response is direct, instructive, challenging and absolute. Jesus knew this man's heart and was willing to make sacrifice and giving to the poor the acid test for this man's eternal destiny. Knowing our hearts, would Jesus ask us the same? What would our response be? Would we pass the test? Would we be willing to give up everything for the sake of the poor? As his followers we *must* love the poor to inherit eternal life. It's not an option. It's a command of Jesus, and we *must* obey everything he has commanded us (Matthew 28:19-20).

Our experience and conviction is that personal motivation begins with personal involvement. Get to know someone who is poor and needy. Jesus surrounded himself with the poor and needy. People in need must become real people to us. They need to become faces with names. They need to become our friends. On that warm summer day in Hyderabad our motivation to help the poor was rekindled because we touched and were touched by real people. And the heart of the matter is that *we* needed to be with them as much as they needed us to help them.

A homeless person, a child in an orphanage, a lonely senior citizen in a nursing home, a sickly person in a hospital—there are many opportunities to get to know people in need. Fix a time, a minimum of once a month, when you will go to visit your "friend" in need. Go on your own, or go with someone else, or even go as a group, but go. Cook a meal for them, celebrate their birthday or just "hang out" with them and listen. Get personally involved! We guarantee it will change your heart, not to mention how it will change their lives! Very often they need friends more than they need money. As you spend time with the poor and needy, think about what it would be like to be in their situation. It will change your perspective for eternity.

Contributors

Guerrimo Adame - lead evangelist, San Diego Church of Christ

Javier & Kelly Amaya - geographic vice presidents of HOPE *worldwide* for Central and South America, based in Mexico City

Eddie & Roxanne Armes - teen ministry leaders, Boston Church of Christ, leaders of HOPE Youth Corps 1995-96

Douglas & Joyce Arthur - evangelist and women's ministry leader, world sector leaders of the Commonwealth sector of the International Churches of Christ, based in Washington, D.C.

Dr. Moe & Amani Bishara - geographic vice presidents of HOPE *worldwide* for the Middle East, based in Beruit, Lebanon

Jim & Donna Blough - world sector administrator for the Commonwealth sector of the International Churches of Christ; administrator for HOPE *worldwide* 1991-93; based in Washington, D.C.

Rodolpho & Lynley Cejas - director and project leader, HOPE *worldwide* Philadelphia

Bud & Kitty Chiles - public relations and fundraising for HOPE for Kids and HOPE *worldwide*, geographic vice presidents of HOPE *worldwide* for Africa, the Caribbean and the eastern United States, based in New York City

Walter Evans - evangelist, Greater Philadelphia Church of Christ, home of HOPE *worldwide*

Robert & Pat Gempel - Robert: chief executive officer of HOPE *worldwide;* Pat: executive vice president of HOPE *worldwide;* based in Philadelphia

Dr. Cameron Gifford - assistant director of Sihanouk Hospital center of HOPE, Phnom Penh, Cambodia

Scott & Lynne Green - evangelist and women's ministry leader, world sector leaders for the China sector of the International Churches of Christ, based in Denver

Douglas Jacoby - evangelist, teacher and author, Washington, D.C. Church of Christ, author of *I Was Hungry*

Steve Johnson - evangelist, world sector leader of the ACES (Africa, Caribbean and eastern United States) sector of the International Churches of Christ, based in New York City

Randy & Jan Jordan - Randy: general counsel for HOPE *worldwide*; both: co-directors of international adoptions for HOPE for Children; based in Washington, D.C.

Erica Kim - woman's ministry leader, world sector leader of the Far East sector of the International Churches of Christ, based in Tokyo, Japan

Phil & Donna Lamb - evangelist and women's ministry leader, world sector leaders for the Central and South America sector of the International Churches of Christ, based in Miami

Dan & Elexa Liu - geographic vice presidents of HOPE *worldwide* for China, based in Hong Kong

Dave Malutinok - financial administrator of HOPE *worldwide,* based in Philadelphia

Kip McKean - world missions evangelist, chairman of the board of HOPE *worldwide,* based in Los Angeles

Randy & Kay McKean - evangelist and women's ministry leader, world sector leaders for the New England and Continental Europe sector of the International Churches of Christ, based in Boston

Drs. Greg & Shelley Metten - elder and women's ministry leader, Los Angeles Church of Christ, director of HOPE for Kids for the Northern Federation

Dr. Stan & Betty Morehead - Stan: physician, regional elder of the Boston Church of Christ; Betty: ministry staff member of the Boston Church of Christ

Mohan & Helen Nanjundan - geographic vice presidents of HOPE *worldwide* for the British Commonwealth, based in Delhi, India

Drs. Graham & Helen Ogle - Graham: director of the Sihanouk Hospital center of HOPE in Phnom Penh, Cambodia; Helen: staff physician at the Sihanouk Hospital center of HOPE

Dr. Mark Ottenweller - director of HOPE *worldwide* AIDS clinic in Johannesburg, South Africa

Mark & Patsy Remijan - geographic vice presidents of HOPE *worldwide* for the Pacific Rim, based in Phnom Penh, Cambodia

Wyndham and Jeanie Shaw - geographic vice presidents of HOPE *worldwide* for New England and Continental Europe, based in Boston

Mike Sheridan - special projects coordinator, HOPE for Kids FundRACE director, HOPE *worldwide* Philadelphia

Mark Templer - lead evangelist, London Church of Christ

Dr. David & Kimi Traver - Dave: physician for HOPE *worldwide* in Phnom Penh, Cambodia; Kimi: program accountant for the Sihanouk Hospital center of HOPE

Dr. Douglas & Joanne Webber - geographic vice presidents of HOPE *worldwide* for Los Angeles; Doug: national director of HOPE for Kids

Shawn & Lena Wooten -geographic vice presidents of HOPE *worldwide* for Commonwealth of Independent States, western U.S. and Canada, based in Moscow

OTHER BOOKS FROM
DISCIPLESHIP PUBLICATIONS INTERNATIONAL

The Daily Power Series
Series Editors: Thomas and Sheila Jones

Thirty Days at the Foot of the Cross
A study of the central issue of Christianity

First...the Kingdom
A study of the Sermon on the Mount

The Mission
The inspiring task of the church in every generation

Teach Us to Pray
A study of the most vital of all spiritual disciplines

To Live Is Christ
An interactive study of the Letter to the Philippians

Glory in the Church
God's plan to shine through his church

The Heart of a Champion
Spiritual inspiration from Olympic athletes

Jesus with the People
Encountering the heart and character of Jesus

Practical Exposition Series

Life to the Full
A study of the writings of James, Peter, John and Jude
by Douglas Jacoby

Mine Eyes Have Seen the Glory
The victory of the Lamb in the Book of Revelation
by Gordon Ferguson

Power in Weakness
Second Corinthians and the Ministry of Paul
by Marty Wooten

The God Who Dared
Genesis: From Creation to Babel
by Douglas Jacoby

The Victory of Surrender
An in-depth study of a powerful biblical concept
(workbook and tapes also available)
by Gordon Ferguson

True and Reasonable
Evidences for God in a skeptical world
by Douglas Jacoby

Raising Awesome Kids in Troubled Times
by Sam and Geri Laing

Friends and Lovers
by Sam and Geri Laing

Friends and Lovers Study Guide
by Mitch and Jan Mitchell

Let It Shine: A Devotional Book for Teens
edited by Thomas and Sheila Jones

Mind Change: The Overcomer's Handbook
by Thomas A. Jones

Especially for Women

She Shall Be Called Woman
Volume I: Old Testament Women
Volume II: New Testament Women
edited by Sheila Jones and Linda Brumley

The Fine Art of Hospitality
edited by Sheila Jones
The Fine Art of Hospitality Handbook
edited by Sheila Jones and Betty Dyson
(two-volume set)

Our Beginning: Genesis Through the Eyes of a Woman
by Kay Summers McKean

For information about ordering these
and many other resources from DPI, call
1-888-DPI-BOOK
or from outside the U.S.
617-938-7396.

World Wide Web
http://www.dpibooks.com